# Diverse Learners in the Classroom

Stuart E. Schwartz
Craig A. Conley
Lisa K. Eaton
*University of Florida*

The McGraw-Hill Companies, Inc.
College Custom Series

*New York  St. Louis  San Francisco  Auckland  Bogotá
Caracas  Lisbon  London  Madrid  Mexico  Milan  Montreal
New Delhi  Paris  San Juan  Singapore  Sydney  Tokyo  Toronto*

**McGraw·Hill**

*A Division of The McGraw·Hill Companies*

Diverse Learners in the Classroom

McGraw-Hill's **College Custom Series** consists of products that are produced from camera-ready copy.
Peer review, class testing, and accuracy are primarily the responsibility of the author(s).

8 9 0 HAM HAM 9 0 9

ISBN 0-07-012550-3

*Editor: Judy T. Ice*
*Printer/Binder: HAMCO/NETPUB Corporation*

# Contents

# Preface: About this Worktext

THE GOAL OF EDUCATION

Children have an innate thirst for knowledge. It is through education that we cultivate children's minds to enable them to accomplish all they would like to accomplish in life. Education enables them to make full use of our potential. All around the world, educational systems and curricula are being reformed to accommodate new trends in society. Whether a child is entirely self-taught or attends public, private, or parochial schools, the goal of education should be to fully develop an individual into a responsible citizen of the world. Such a citizen understands and appreciates the full range of human thought, recognizing that truth and knowledge may take many different forms and may be approached from a multiplicity of perspectives.

> **VOICES OF EXPERIENCE**
>
> *"Education is not just another consumer item. It is the bedrock of our democracy."*
> —Mary Hatwood Futrell, educator

WHO SHOULD USE THIS WORKTEXT

*Teaching Diverse Learners* is designed for students in all disciplines who are studying to become teachers. Future teachers will face classrooms full of diverse learners, some exhibiting intellectual and learning differences, some having physical and health-related differences, and some expressing behavior and personality differences. Other learners will have economic advantages and disadvantages, be coming to terms with their sexual orientation, and be of racially, ethnically, and religiously diverse backgrounds. Future teachers need to be comfortable and effective in interacting with *everyone* in the classroom.

SPECIAL FEATURES

Through high-interest, realistic scenarios, this worktext innovatively demonstrates the realities of human diversity in the classroom. The numerous first-person accounts, empowerment tips, and classroom strategies encountered in the textbook ensure that future teachers are motivated to increase their comfort level around students who are different (as well as their parents). The activities encourage future teachers to examine their own personal biases and find ways to embrace unity in diversity.

This worktext is a springboard to further study. You can explore the world of diversity "at your fingertips" via the Exceptional People World Wide Web Homepage, an interactive gateway to global diversity internet sites [www.coe.ufl.edu/DiverseWorld/].

For more information or for assistance with human diversity courses or workshops, contact:

Stuart E. Schwartz, Ed.D.
University of Florida
P.O. Box 117050
Gainesville, FL 32611-7050

office: 352-392-0701 x258
fax: 352-392-2655
e-mail: stuart_schwartz@qm.server.ufl.edu
homepage: www.coe.ufl.edu/DiverseWorld/

For more information on other human diversity books and support materials, contact:

Judy Ice
McGraw-Hill, Inc.
6512 Six Forks Road, Suite 602
Raleigh, NC 27615

office: 919-870-1311
fax: 919-870-1314
e-mail: judyice@aol.com

# Introduction: The Classroom Microcosm

THE WORLD IS
A CLASSROOM

Classrooms are microcosms. They are small worlds where hierarchies are established, plans laid and carried out, competitions held, and personal relationships formed. There is, in fact, no border between the classroom and the world—they are one. The world is a larger classroom in which every moment is a learning experience of one kind or another. Children come to the classroom with all those experiences, and the learning which occurs in a room in a building is but one more kind, and often not the most compelling kind.

It is not the job of schools to teach children how to think about their fellow human beings. Society pays lip service to the concept of mutual respect, but we usually offer no specific rules or information to make that respect a reality. If we said "Mathematics is good and useful, and children should practice it," but then left it to happen spontaneously, most people would never learn math.

When we enter a classroom, as student or teacher, we come as we are. Our age, race, religion, culture, sexual orientation, physical health, language, and ability to learn in the prescribed way do not alter from what they are in the larger world. If that classroom is a place where the reality of who we are is denied, it will be very difficult for us to learn anything much beyond the fear and cynicism behind that denial. If intolerance is institutionalized, then what children will learn about the world in the classroom will color their attitudes negatively forever.

Life in the larger world is fast and busy, and too often people act on their habit of hate, fear, and ignorant reaction to anything percieved as different. The classroom is, for designated time periods, a more static place, where a diverse population comes together

> **VOICES OF EXPERIENCE**
>
> *"When those who have the power to name and to socially construct reality choose not to see you or hear you, whether you are dark-skinned, old, disabled, female, or speak in a different accent or dialect than theirs, when someone with the authority of a teacher, say, describes the world and you are not in it, there is a moment of psychic disequilibrium, as if you looked into a mirror and saw nothing."*
> —Adrienne Rich, poet

regularly for the stated purpose of putting its attention on learning and understanding. The classroom offers students an opportunity to add to the knowledge each person needs about his or her fellow humans. The classroom also compels teachers to impart this knowledge if they, in fact, want to teach anything at all of substance. That's because when the celebration of the diversity is left out of the classroom, myriad barriers to learning are introduced. When students learn to look at others with respect and gain an appreciation for people's uniqueness, they measurably grow in their own abilities because they gain confidence in themselves and strength from the support of others.

GUIDING PRINCIPLES

Author and educator Herbert Kohl (1994) has advised today's teachers to follow three interesting principles: "hopemongering," "not-learning," and "creative maladjustment." Hopemongering, he says, "is the affirmation of hope and the dream of a just and equitable future despite all the contrary evidence provided by experience." The classroom teacher who is a hopemonger does not despair about society's shortcomings but rather teaches by example that, one person at a time, we can keep the ideals of equality and respect alive. Kohl describes not-learning as "the conscious decision not to learn something that you could learn. It consists, for example, of refusing to learn how to cheat on your taxes, cook crack cocaine, or yield to community pressure to become racist or sexist—choosing not to learn something that you find morally offensive or personally noxious." The classroom teacher who practices not-learning will foster independence, integrity, and critical thinking in his or her students. Perhaps most important is the last principle—creative maladjustment. "Creative maladjustment," Kohl says, "is the art of not becoming what other people want you to be and learning, in difficult times, to affirm yourself while at the same time remaining caring and compassionate" (p. xiii). The classroom teacher who introduces creative-maladjustment will help to promote empowered citizens who will be equipped to bring about positive change in our diverse society through a fuller expression of their own potential.

In order to teach any skill, three vital steps are necessary. The first step is to decide that the skill is valuable. The second step is to agree upon the best methods for teaching the skill. The third step is to work on your own understanding so that you, as a teacher, can teach by deed as well as by word. It is by our own belief in a subject, by our own enthusiasm for its importance and meaning, that we communicate best. The goal of this worktext is to spark your enthusiasm for the richness of human diversity and encourage you to communicate that enthusiasm to your students.

REFERENCES    Kohl, H.  (1994).  *I won't learn from you, and other thoughts on creative maladjustment.*  New York: The New Press.

# Human Diversity in the Classroom

OBJECTIVES  By the end of this chapter you should be able to answer these questions:

- What are four ways you can teach your students about diversity by your own example?
- What are two reasons students tend to subdivide in the classroom?
- What constitutes an "exceptional" individual?
- How have attitudes about human diversity changed over time?
- What are the three crucial criteria of labels we use?

THE CLASSROOM IS A MICROCOSM

*Imagine that on the first day of a new school year you arrive in class to find seated before you fifteen sets of twins. It would never occur to you to teach them as if there were only fifteen students present. Clearly there are thirty students, each an individual with a distinct personality, learning style, and approach to life. Though fifteen sets of individuals look alike, have the same racial, ethnic, cultural, national, and religious backgrounds, speak the same languages, live in the same neighborhoods, eat the same foods, and share attitudes which they have been taught by their parents, you would never assume that their needs were exactly the same, or that they would perform equally well or poorly academically, or that they would behave the same way in similar situations.*

INTRODUCTION

Just as no two twins are exactly alike, every single person we come across in our lives is a unique individual. We are *all* diverse people, with special talents, different experiences, original ideas, and personal viewpoints. Look around at ten people sitting near you. Notice their faces and their clothing styles. Now "guesstimate" the answers to the following questions:

- How many of those ten people are foreign born?  _____

- How many belong to a minority religious group?  _____

- How many are living with a chronic illness?  _____

- How many have learning disabilities?  _____

- How many are battling drug or alcohol abuse?  _____

- How many are homosexual or bisexual?  _____

Using statistics from a 1994 Department of Education report, two of those people will be foreign born, two will have a speech problem, and one will be a member of a minority religious group. If your random sampling includes persons with children, two children will have learning disabilities, two will face future drug or alcohol abuse, one will be mentally retarded, and at least one will be homosexual.

PERSPECTIVE
ONE

Every individual is unique, but students in the classroom like to sub-divide sometimes, feeling that they belong in the same category as some, and not as others. Why might they tend to focus on differences?

_____

_____

Focusing on differences may make them feel secure as part of a small group, or they may feel uncomfortable or awkward with people who are different. Whenever their reactions to another are based on gender, race, physical or mental disability, sexual orientation, religion, economic class, or any other category, they are cheating themselves of opportunities to benefit from that individual and are cheating that person of his or her right to participate fully in the classroom.

Most of us have found ourselves uncomfortable at one time or another in dealing with someone we perceive to be different. For example, we may feel unsure of how to talk to someone from another culture, we may have incorrect expectations regarding an individual with a different skin color, we may have difficulty having a relaxed conversation with a person of a different sexual orientation, or we may find ourselves staring at someone who looks different due to an injury or a disability. In order to improve our interactions, increase our self-understanding, and teach respect for diversity to our students, we need to know what human differences are, examine some of their causes, and reduce our myths and misunderstandings about people who are diverse. Since every one of us fits into many categories of diversity, we severely impoverish our lives if we limit our interaction through ignorance.

> **VOICES OF EXPERIENCE**
>
> *"Minorities are individuals or groups of individuals especially qualified. The masses are the collection of people not specially qualified."*
> *—José Ortega y Gasset, philosopher*

This worktext should help you to understand exactly how to define human differences and give you some guidance in regard to social interaction within a diverse classroom. It includes helpful exercises and activities which will give you insights into other perspectives and will help you to develop sensitivity and self-awareness so that you can effectively teach your students to treat all people respectfully and fairly. Knowledge allows us to live and respond based on facts rather than myths. Information is the key to interacting with others with tolerance and respect, which is a challenge most teachers want to meet.

PERSPECTIVE
TWO

As we noted earlier, no two people are alike. Yet sometimes a person stands out in one or more ways from those who seem to be "average." This person could, of course, be anyone, depending upon the group to which he or she is being compared. Historically, Caucasian, heterosexual, English speakers have not been considered exceptional in the United States. However, in some parts of our country now, Spanish is the predominant language, so English speakers are the ones who are different. In many communities Hispanic or African American families outnumber Caucasian families, so it is exceptional to be Caucasian there. In a group of mostly females, it is exceptional to be male.

The expectations that a certain population has upon its members for specific behaviors or group standards also affect whether the individual is considered different. A group of teens which expects its friends to dress in a specific style might consider anyone who dresses differently to be exceptional. Parents who have high academic expectations for their child might consider C's to be exceptional grades, while other parents might find those grades "average" and acceptable. How we are viewed and accepted depends largely upon the situation in which we find ourselves.

Just as a group's expectations affect its members, teachers' expectations affect the members of their classrooms. Teachers' biases inevitably shape their interactions with students. A good example of this "expectation phenomenon" is the study conducted by Rosenthal and Jacobson (1968). All third grade students and teachers in one district were randomly divided into two equal sets. One set of teachers was told that its students would exhibit terrible behavior and low intelligence. The other set was told that its students would exhibit model behavior and high intelligence. Rosenthal and Jacobson found that the students in the first set demonstrated inappropriate behaviors and had poor academic performance. The students in the second set exhibited very few behavior problems and had high academic performance. This study demonstrated that a teacher's expectations can profoundly affect student performance in the classroom.

Answer the following set of questions (adapted from Bosworth, 1995) to see if any of your expectations might be governed by biases.

True or False:

1. _____ Asian-Americans are model students because they all work hard to excel in school.
2. _____ Caucasian students are affected by their ethnic background.
3. _____ For most immigrant students, education is not a priority.
4. _____ African American students have difficulty in school because they are verbal learners.
5. _____ All Hispanic students speak Spanish.
6. _____ Native American students are quiet by nature.
7. _____ You should speak up when talking to a student in a wheelchair.
8. _____ Gay or lesbian students are usually identifiable by their behavior, dress, or speech.
9. _____ The majority of students with learning disabilities are boys.
10. _____ Academic excellence comes easily to gifted students.

(Answers: 1. F, 2. T, 3. F, 4. F, 5. F, 6. F, 7. F, 8. F, 9. T, 10. F)

Once you identify your personal biases, you can build a supportive classroom atmosphere where differences are not overlooked or minimized but rather are explored, discussed, and celebrated (Bosworth, 1995).

Some diverse individuals have disabilities which inhibit or prevent their participation in some activities or interfere with their learning. Some have special gifts or talents which make them different. And some have both talents and disabilities. Although exceptional people differ from others in some major or minor way, they are individuals *first*. Their exceptionality is only one of their characteristics. They each have their own unique goals, dreams, hopes, and needs.

Many of us may think of disabilities as physical limitations. A disability may indeed be physical, but it may also be emotional, cognitive, or sensory in nature. A physical disability may or may not require one to use a wheelchair or other assistive device. Most people with vision or hearing impairments can easily correct their conditions with eyeglasses or hearing aids. You can see that individuals with both visible and hidden disabilities live and function independently in every part of society every day.

In order to speak about human diversity with any real meaning, then, we would need to consider every possible difference from the norm, every possible norm, and every possible level of expectation. That is clearly impractical if not impossible. However, we can look at the most common types of diversity which you are likely to encounter in your classroom. These selected categories should enable you to have a thorough understanding of these areas of exceptionality and should help you to be a better teacher of students who may, from time to time or from group to group, be considered different.

You yourself may now or in the future belong to a group which is characterized as exceptional. What are six things that make you unique? Number them in order of importance.

_____  _____  _____

_____  _____  _____

You may be unique due to such factors as your race, gender, sexual orientation, intelligence level, size, age, religion, talents, or socioeconomic class. An understanding of the fact that the perception of diversity shifts constantly depending upon time and place will help you to avoid the insensitivity that comes from ignorance. This worktext should help you, as well, to have a better understanding of yourself as an exceptional person in our complex society. With this knowledge, you can then serve as a role-model to your students.

PERSPECTIVE
THREE

Each category of diversity has, of course, had its own unique history. We can, however, speak in broad terms about some aspects of the acceptance and treatment of exceptional people in the past. For example, we know that the teachings of all the world's major religions include references to those who are sick, weak, unfortunate, or disadvantaged. Confucius, Buddha, Mohammed, and Jesus all wrote or spoke about the need to show compassion. The sacred texts of the great religions all advocate humane and sympathetic treatment for every individual.

However, in many cases and in all cultures, exceptionality has been associated with sinfulness. It was looked upon as a kind of curse or punishment, either because of a lack of faith or because of some failure in the individual or in his or her parents. This mistaken attitude has fundamentally colored society's perception of differences, and even today the attitude has not entirely been dispelled.

> **VOICES OF EXPERIENCE**
>
> *"Educational institutions have traditionally viewed any deviation from the norm as a compromise in academic excellence. As a result, any change in perspective due to diversity in our society is resisted"*
> —*Maricopa Community College*

Since earliest recorded history there have been instances of humane treatment of those who were different or disabled. In Athens, around 600 BC, a famous lawgiver named Solon designed a system for providing care for soldiers who had been disabled in war. However, Solon's attitude was uncommonly enlightened. In the Middle Ages, the lives of exceptional people were often full of suffering, and customarily they benefited from little or no support from society. Both Martin Luther and John Calvin, important Christian reformers in the sixteenth century, stated their belief that disabled individuals had no souls and that therefore society had no responsibility to them at all. Those who were deaf, mentally retarded, epileptic, and blind, as well as some especially gifted or talented individuals, were often thought to be possessed by demons and sometimes were subjected to exorcisms to purge the "devils" from them.

> **VOICES OF EXPERIENCE**
>
> *"Educational institutions, like any other segment of American institutional life, must **embrace diversity**. Why? Because it is the rational, logical, and intellectual thing to do given the changes in our society. To do otherwise is to continue to insulate ourselves from the very society we are charged with serving."*
> —Maricopa Community College

The 18th and 19th centuries brought the beginning of efforts to educate and to care for exceptional people. There was more treatment for people who were mentally ill and mentally retarded, and programs were instituted to educate people who were deaf, mute, and blind. Special schools for special conditions—such as asylums for people who were blind—began to be established in the United States as well as in Europe. Programs within public schools in the United States were begun in the early 1990s, segregating exceptional children into special classes apart from the main student body. Since that time, programs for students with special needs have steadily grown and developed, with an emphasis on inclusion rather than exclusion.

While there have been flashes of enlightened attitudes and actions toward human diversity throughout history, in general our treatment of individuals with differences has been shameful. In every period of history so far, and in virtually all cultures, there has been a stigma attached to difference. Societies have neglected, persecuted, and sometimes exterminated those of its members who exhibited noticeable variations from the perceived norm. Since perception is always subject to change, and all of us fall into many categories of exceptionality, it behooves us to continue to grow in humanity and in understanding. The best way to do that is to educate ourselves and pass that knowledge on. Intolerance is the direct result of ignorance.

The on-going enactment of human rights legislation and the increasing awareness of the contributions of diverse people to our society gives hope that we may be entering a new century in which differences are not only recognized and tolerated but appreciated and honored. In the past two decades there has been phenomenal progress in the fields of medicine and technology. We must continually redefine exceptionality due to increased understanding of the causes of some categories of exceptionality, medical advances in the cure and treatment of some conditions, and new technology which enables people to function despite previously limiting conditions. It is an exciting time to be studying the subject of human diversity.

> **VOICES OF EXPERIENCE**
>
> *"Schools are complex places. The more closely they are examined, the more complex they become."*
> —Kathryn Whitmore, professor

PERSPECTIVE
FOUR

The terms you use to describe or identify students who are different should be positive, current, and correct. The goal is not to expand the lexicon of political correctness. But it is important to think carefully about the words you use. You can probably think of many inappropriate terms which have been used to identify people with diverse qualities. The acceptability of terms changes with time, and a word may be the term of choice of one group or individual and be offensive to another.

For example, some people with hearing impairments prefer to be described as "hearing impaired," yet the National Theater For The Deaf uses the term "deaf." The best way to be sure that you are not giving offense is to go to the expert. Ask a friend or colleague who is an exceptional person, or who has a close relationship with someone who is, what is most acceptable to them.

Labels serve an important purpose. They are the way we attempt to identify and describe people. They allow us to distinguish characteristics which may facilitate communication among professionals. For example, psychologists and educators may use labels to discuss the special needs of an individual or of a group of people. On the other hand, labeling may stigmatize a person, contribute to low self-esteem, and cause him or her to suffer discrimination. Once labels are applied to someone, particularly by an official evaluator such as a doctor, teacher, or psychologist, it may be difficult to ever remove the label. Consequently, we should carefully give consideration to the accuracy of those labels and to their potential short- and long-term effects.

In any culture, some labels are generally thought to be positive and others negative. Most of us would have a positive reaction to the label "intelligent," but we might have very different ideas what we mean by that label. Some of us say our dogs are intelligent if they can roll over, for instance. In American culture, "overweight" is usually a negative label, but a fashion model might be called overweight even though, by the standards of the society, she is thin. Words have different connotations, or meanings, for different groups, and the effect of labeling, as we have seen, can differ from person to person. The best guideline is to always remember that the person comes first and the label simply identifies a specific characteristic about that person. For instance, don't say "Moslems practice beautiful traditions," but rather "People of the Muslim faith practice beautiful traditions."

EMPOWERMENT TIPS

Can you improve the attitudes of your students toward exceptional individuals? You certainly can by being a good model. The guidelines suggested below should assist you in your efforts to improve your interactions with diverse people, and they should serve as excellent examples for students who observe your behaviors. By interacting correctly and comfortably, you will greatly aid those people who are uncomfortable or afraid due to ignorance, myths, and misconceptions.

* *Tell your students about differences.* Encourage students to ask questions as their curiosity is quite normal. If students are given correct information in a matter of fact manner, they will perceive that being different is not mysterious or something to fear. People tend to fear that which is unknown, so it is critically important to teach students about human diversity so that all possible fears about exceptionalities are eliminated.

* *Expect normal behaviors and achievement from diverse individuals.* If you think that a nonnative speaker of English or a student with a hearing impairment will be unable to score well on a test, you will be hampering the success of that person. If you expect that a student with mental retardation can never learn to ride a subway, you are setting a major roadblock in the way of that person's learning to use public transportation. The expectations of influential people, such as parents, teachers, and friends, have a strong effect on students' confidence level and motivation to achieve. The potential of people

who are diverse is usually only limited by the opportunities to learn and the inappropriately low expectations of significant others.

- *Always display your respect and comfort.* It is important for you to set a good example. If you interact with all students in a respectful manner, and if it appears that you are comfortable in your interactions with everyone, your entire class and fellow teachers will follow your lead. Remember that others will copy your behaviors.

- *Stop people who are ridiculing or joking about people who are diverse.* If someone begins to ridicule or joke about an exceptional individual, challenge that person to stop. If you sit there and laugh along with the crowd, you are just as guilty as the joke teller. By participating you are giving the impression that you condone such negative behavior. It takes guts to put your foot down, but if you do so in a serious and positive manner, others will no doubt respect you for having the courage of your convictions. Comments such as, "Excuse me, but the racist joke you are telling is making me uncomfortable," or "If you don't mind I'd appreciate your saving any jokes about male-bashing for a time when I'm not around" will usually work.

- *Be yourself around those who stand out as different.* Putting on an act around people who are different will be recognized as patronizing or demeaning behavior. It is not necessary for you to sprint ahead and open a door for someone in a wheelchair unless you usually do that for everyone. If you are taking a leisurely walk and normally say hello to people you meet, then by all means say hello to that person with a guide dog who is walking by. If you usually ignore people whom you don't know, and you don't know that person with an oxygen tank, then ignore him or her as well. Diverse people want to be treated like everyone else, and they can tell when you are acting.

- *Use everyday vocabulary.* The vocabulary you commonly use should be fine with anyone you meet. With people who are blind it is appropriate to say, "It's nice to see you," or "Isn't it a beautiful day?" It is acceptable to say to a friend of yours who uses a wheelchair, "Let's take a walk to the park." People who are different use common, everyday language all the time, so don't feel the least bit awkward using your everyday vocabulary. If you stop to think about the "right" words to use, you will come across as uncomfortable and the substitute words you select will probably be wrong.

- *Suggest activities in which you are interested.* If you like tennis, ask your friend who has epilepsy to play. If you are going to a theme park, invite your friend who is a Buddhist to accompany you. If you want to go to an art museum, don't hesitate to invite your friend who is visually impaired along. Diverse students should not be excluded from activities just because you think those activities would not be appropriate for them. Ask your friends who are diverse to participate. They are fully capable of selecting the activities which they will enjoy and which fit their interests.

- *Look at but never stare at someone who is different.* It is fine to look, note any differences in your mind, and then go on with your interaction with an exceptional person in a normal fashion. Staring at someone who is dressed differently, or disfigured, or short statured is rude and will make that person feel uncomfortable. Some diverse people will stare right back or will bluntly ask you why you are staring. It is very appropriate, however, to look in a normal fashion at people who appear different with whom you are interacting. Avoiding eye contact, or looking away, is just as rude as staring.

- *Talk to the person and not just to his or her companion.* When interacting with a person who is with a family member or companion, be sure to address the person rather than the family member or companion. A person from another country can usually answer questions or respond appropriately in conversation without assistance. Likewise, if you are with a friend who has a disability, don't respond for the friend. When put in that situation, such as a waiter asking you what your companion would like to eat, don't respond for your friend. Politely suggest to the waiter that he or she should ask your friend. Although that situation may be a bit uncomfortable, it will be a good experience for that insensitive restaurant employee.

CLASSROOM STRATEGIES

As you model appropriate interactions for your students, think of diversity as a process of acknowledging differences through action (Maricopa Community Colleges, 1996). In the classroom, this involves welcoming heterogeneity by developing strategies at the interpersonal level. The following classroom strategies (adapted from Bosworth, 1995) were developed by educators working with specific student populations:

- Practice treating all students the same regardless of their differences. It is important not to afford too many or too few accommodations or modifications based on a student's difference. Expect the best from *all* students and create an environment which will ensure success for all types of students.

- Get to know students as individuals; avoid expectations based upon biases, myths, or stereotypes. Learn about what is going on in your students' lives both inside and outside the school walls. Visiting different neighborhoods around the school is a good way to observe the lives of your students. Find where your students "hang out" after school. Locate nearby churches and libraries.

* Carefully balance academic content with instructional processes. Every student in your classroom will learn differently. Some may learn best by hearing new information, some by reading, and some by observing. Teachers must incorporate a variety of teaching styles so that all students have a chance to succeed.

* Use group work to foster teamwork and build understanding. Utilize students' uniqueness to enhance communication, problem-solving, and decision-making skills. When students are encouraged or required to work on class projects together, they learn about each other as individuals, thereby dispelling negative attitudes and stereotypes.

* Involve parents. Think of your students' parents as a large staff of teaching assistants. When parents encourage and reinforce education, their children's academic success soars. If you make an effort to include parents in decision-making and academic planning, they will provide a much needed support for classroom success.

* Build on what students already know. Use newspapers and guest speakers from the community to help connect lessons with examples from life. Encourage students to openly and freely share their own experiences with the class.

* Celebrate the richness of divergent cultures, experiences, and perspectives. Plan a culture day in the classroom or the school. Choose a theme, such as traditional music, folk art, or cooking, and focus on two or three cultures with interesting similarities and differences. Allow students time to interact, ask questions, and sample the different cultures.

* Teach the *Platinum Rule*: "Treat others as you wish to be treated."

Finally, let's return to the scenario that opened this chapter. Read the situation below and record your reactions. Answering the questions will help prepare you to handle diversity in the classroom. There is no one "right" answer, so be thoughtful and be yourself.

|  |  |
|---|---|
| Setting: | The hallway outside your classroom |
| Time: | A few minutes after school has ended |
| Person involved: | Betty, the mother of twin students in your class |
| Background: | Betty dresses the twins alike and is fond of claiming that they are "identical in every way." |
| Circumstances: | You have met Betty in the hallway the day after the twins received back their first graded test |
| Simulation: | Betty says to you, "I simply cannot believe that my twins did not make the same score on this test. They studied the same amount of time, they read the same material, and I drilled them together. Excuse my bluntness, but I can only blame you for this discrepancy." |

1. What is your objective?

_____

_____

_____

2. What do you say to Betty?

_____

_____

_____

3. What will you say to the twins?

_____

_____

_____

_____

Consider your attitude toward people who are different. When you meet someone in a wheelchair, how do you react? How do you feel?

_____

What about someone who speaks with a heavy accent or who uses gestures and sign language for communication?

_____

What about a street person? How do you react?

_____

How do you feel when you see two men or two women dancing together? Are you uncomfortable? Do you try to avoid those people?

_____

As a role model to your students, the attitudes that you display toward people who are different is critical.

Attitudes are learned early in life when children interact with others and observe the human interactions of family members and friends. The child who hears his or her parents or teachers make negative remarks about diverse people, or who observes playmates ridicule and tease other children who are different, will probably be greatly influenced by these experiences. The child who grows up in an environment where individual differences are noted and treated with respect will more likely not have negative expectations, feelings of discomfort, or negative attitudes.

REFERENCES        Bosworth, K. (1995). Cultural diversity in the classrooms. In *Teacher Talk* [On-line]. Available: http://educ/indiana.edu/cas/tt/v2i2/cultural.html

Maricopa Community Colleges. (1996). Working descriptions of diversity. In *Diversity defined* [On-line]. Available: http://www.emc.maricopa.edu/diversity/overview.html

Rosenthal, R. & Jacobson, L. (1968). *Pygmalion in the classroom*. New York: Holt, Rinehard, & Winston.

# Diverse Cultures in the Classroom

**OBJECTIVES**

By the end of this chapter you should be able to answer these questions:

- Why is multicultural education important?
- How is cultural identity determined?
- How is cultural identity passed along from one generation to the next?
- What is the role of the teacher in this process?
- How does cultural diversity manifest itself in the classroom?
- What benefits can accrue from the cultural diversity of a class?
- How can you more effectively teach a culturally diverse class?

**THE CLASSROOM IS A MICROCOSM**

*You are eating lunch in the school cafeteria, your back to the table behind you, when you hear some students talking. They are unaware of you, but you recognize the voices of two of your class leaders. A newly enrolled student, Billy, approaches their table, asking if he can join them. "No way, man, these seats are all taken," the first student responds, in a nasty tone. Billy, muttering his apologies for asking, retreats to another table. The students laugh loudly, and you hear Bryan, the first boy, say "I can't stand that brown-noser. All he does is suck up to the teachers." "Yeah," the second replies, imitating Billy's Southern drawl, "Yes, Ma'am; no, Ma'am; excuse me, Sir!"*

**INTRODUCTION**

People frequently misuse the term *culture* to mean civilization. Culture, however, is not a synonym for civilization. We can think of civilization as a universal quality inherent in all people. In other words, we all have the ability to behave in a civilized manner, exhibiting compassion and practicing cooperation. Culture, on the other hand, is a subjective—rather than a universal—human quality. A culture is made up of the ideas, customs, skills, arts, interests, and emotions of a people. By communicating and

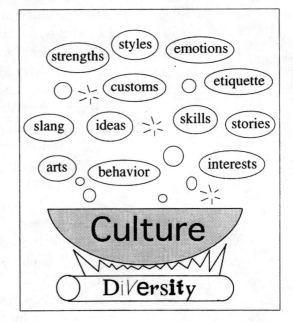

15

passing along these ideas and customs to our children, we allow our culture to survive.

Civilization is a "social climate in which people in differing groups can deal with each other in ways that respect cultural differences" (Cleveland, 1994). Diversity strengthens our species and adds threads to the tapestry of our lives. It exponentially increases the possibilities for progress and positive change in the world because, rather than seeing from only one point of view, it allows us to see from many. We would be sadly diminished if the music of the universe consisted of only one note. We would be even more sadly diminished if people were free of differences. Too often we speak of tolerating difference when we should always be respecting and celebrating it. Teachers have a vitally important role in communicating the value of diversity to our students.

Sometimes science fiction films and books portray a world where diversity has been limited or eradicated. Without exception, those images are frightening in their sameness and colorlessness. We recoil from the prospect because we instinctively know that to destroy difference is to destroy our own individuality—the very thing which makes us feel human—our uniqueness. The lesson we must keep learning and teaching is that only by respecting and honoring the difference in others can we preserve our own. The English poet John Donne wrote, "Every man's death diminishes me." The corollary to that truth is that everyone's difference enhances me.

PERSPECTIVE ONE

Teachers, second perhaps only to parents, play a vital role in the process of cultural transmission. All cultures have a history and a heritage which is carefully handed down. Cultures are identifiable because they share certain characteristics. People within the group have ways of telling who is and who is not a member. Members share a language through which cultural interactions take place, certain group values are shared, and various social and behavioral patterns are followed. Members follow special rules of etiquette when communicating with others, introducing themselves to strangers, getting someone's attention, and leave-taking, for example.

> **VOICES OF EXPERIENCE**
>
> *"Culture is not life in its entirety, but just the moment of security, strength, and clarity."*
> —José Ortega y Gasset, philosopher

Members of each culture also have their own unique slang expressions and figures of speech. You can learn more about these codes of behavior and expression by asking what is appropriate in certain situations. However, some of these rules may not be meant for general public knowledge. Such cultural interactions are often kept private so that members of the specific community may identify

16

outsiders easily (Bienvenu & Colonomos, 1993). Can you think of some "culture codes" that teachers use? How do you identify other educators? Give examples of a special language of teachers.

_____

_____

Students and teachers use words such as *period, semester,* and *term* to describe increments of time, for instance.

What are some identifying examples of American culture?

_____

_____

Examples of American culture could be anything from the Statue of Liberty, to baseball, to apple pie. What are some ways in which we pass on the values and customs of a culture?

_____

_____

The celebration of holidays in honor of heroes such as Martin Luther King, Jr. or George Washington and the observance of significant dates in history such as the Fourth of July or President's Day are culturally bonding experiences. What are some other cultural icons?

_____

_____

Examples of American cultural icons are as different as John Wayne and Louis Armstrong, or Mardi Gras and the Macy's Parade.

PERSPECTIVE
TWO
Thinking of some of the symbols of America which are recognizable to people in other nations is one way to start considering how we are identified by our culture. Corporate symbols such as Mickey Mouse®, Coca Cola®, and CNN® are known around the world. Do they define part of American culture? Do they, in any way, define you as an American?

_____

_____

17

You can see that cultural identity is very complex. Remember that individuals may not accept all the symbols of their culture any more than you do. What are some cultural symbols which you recognize from other cultures?

_____

_____

_____

African dress styles and printed fabrics are distinctive, as are the silks of Indian saris and the woven designs of Native American art. These and other symbols such as Reggae or sitar music and Navajo or Eskimo art have been widely adopted by the world population in general, but still retain their cultural associations for us.

PERSPECTIVE
THREE

Issues of cultural diversity arise in every classroom, regardless of what the racial or ethnic makeup may be. As Julie James, a high school teacher, observed, "You have a diverse classroom. The fact that your students all have a similar cultural heritage does not mean that they are all the same. Yes, students often dress like their friends or bond into constellations of 'like personalities,' but given the chance, most high school students will assert their differences. The key is giving them a chance. The challenge to the teacher is being able to consistently recognize and value the creative ways that students express themselves and to use these actions, words, or habits to talk about diversity issues" (1995, p. 2).

Students come to school with a set of values which need to be recognized and explored. Classroom rules should reflect the value you place on diversity and your respect for all cultures. At the same time, you should maintain a climate for learning. How can you make this happen? List three strategies below:

_____

_____

_____

It is necessary first to acknowledge differences rather than ignoring them or minimizing them. When you begin by recognizing and respecting individual differences, it is easy and natural to move on to the exploration of national and cultural differences among the students (Covert, 1996).

PERSPECTIVE
FOUR

In anthropology, important distinctions are made between "ideal" and "real" culture (Arvizu, Snyder, & Espinosa, 1980). Ideal culture refers to what people say they believe or how they think they should behave. Aspects of ideal culture are frequently expressed in proverbs, stories, myths, and jokes. These may contrast sharply with the real culture, which is how individuals actually behave in specific situations. What are some ways that you can use this aspect of culture to promote understanding among students?

_____

_____

Incorporating the reading or telling of these stories, myths, and tales is a useful way of drawing attention to cultural diversity in the classroom. Can you think of some examples of songs and stories from your own childhood?

_____

_____

Comparison of these popular tales often shows the similarities underlying superficial differences.

Some elements of culture operate at a conscious level of awareness, whereas others do not. Implicit (covert) culture includes elements hidden or taken for granted to the extent that they are not easily observable or consciously recognized by individuals. Attitudes, fears, values, religious beliefs, and assumptions are common elements of implicit culture.

Explicit (overt) culture, on the other hand, is visible and can be described verbally. This includes speech, tools, styles of dress, and concrete behaviors.

> **VOICES OF EXPERIENCE**
>
> *"The choice of a point of view is the initial act of a culture."*
> —José Ortega y Gasset, philosopher

Keeping covert culture in mind, Gordon and Roberts (1991) developed some valuable guidelines for teachers of diverse students. They suggested that all subject matter content should be culturally inclusive, incorporating opposing opinions and divergent interpretations.

It should represent both diversity and unity within and across cultures. It is important to stress depth rather than breadth. It is also important to treat subject matter as tentative because it is socially constructed, as is all knowledge, and to endeavor to build on the knowledge and experience of all students. Understanding is fostered by the examination of controversy and by mutual learning, so that interactive teaching rather than rote learning is required (Gordon and Roberts, 1991).

PERSPECTIVE
FIVE

Having made distinctions between ideal, real, overt, and covert cultures, it must be noted that the scientific theories of culture do not always pertain to the realities of people who live together. When we examine particular cultures up close, we find that the individuals do not necessarily share beliefs and ways of life. What else might tie people together, then? As social scientist Amelie Rorty (1995) notes, a group of people may be held together by the joys of arguing with one another, even about the most fundamental issues! "How finely, at what level of generality do a people share customs, dress, music, and so on?" Rorty asks. "In many cultures, men and women, the young and the elderly, priests and merchants, the high and low born do not have the same practices or concepts. They may recognize—and be committed to—their practical, economic interdependence, but they often sincerely profess not to understand one another; and they often identify themselves by their internal contrasts, rather than by their alleged presumptively shared culture" (1995, p. 161). Many people are quick to identify themselves with a particular culture, but we shouldn't lose sight of how much diversity exists within even the smallest of groups.

According to Harland Cleveland (1994), president of the World Academy of Art and Science, no single culture is or can be complete in itself. Cultures keep redefining themselves, he explains, by mixing and matching with other cultures, "not only through getting to know people who look, act, and believe differently but through exposure in a more open electronic world to new faiths and fashions, new lifestyles, workways, technologies, clothing, and cuisines" (1994, p. 756). Every culture, then, is in a constant state of flux. "But many millions of people in this time of uncertainty and insecurity believe that their best haven of certainty and security is a group based on ethnic similarity, common faith, economic interest, or political likemindedness," Cleveland says. "The fear that drives people to cleave to such 'primordial loyalties' makes it harder for them to learn behaviors consistent with tolerance of others who may be guided by different faiths and loyalties" (1994, p. 756).

The only way to fight such fear is to avoid uncritical, narrow-minded thinking. In the words of Danny Weil, an expert on multiculturalism and critical thinking, the way to begin to think fair-mindedly and critically is to exercise reciprocity. Reciprocity simply means "to imaginatively place oneself in the 'shoes' of others often diverse in thought from ourselves, to consider strengths and weaknesses of opposing cultural and political points of view, and to overcome our sometimes egocentric tendencies to wed ourselves blindly and uncritically to one belief or another without the benefit of self-examination and critical analysis" (1993, p. 211).

The first step to overcoming egocentrism is to ask yourself these key questions (Derived from Weil, 1993):

❧ How do I arrive at my conclusions and choices?

_____

_____

❧ Upon what assumptions do I base my inferences?

_____

_____

❧ What evidence do I have to support my beliefs?

_____

_____

❧ What other points of view inform the bank of data and evidence I use to support my assumptions and consequent decisions and actions?

_____

_____

Uncritical thinking, Weil explains, is inherited from secondary sources, such as television, movies, parents, friends, institutions, and teachers. "The uncritical mind looks for stereotypes and simplistic categories in which to conveniently place people, things, and places. . . . Without the benefit of critical reasoning within and about diverse cultural points of view, the human mind becomes at peace with internalized cultural stereotypes, falsehoods, prejudices, and biases, and can accomplish little to help transform the world lived in and with others." In other words, the uncritical mind cannot fully participate in or take advantage of another culture, much less its own.  If we are to succeed in living and thriving together as human beings with diverse cultures, "we must become actively engaged in dialogue about diversity, with an interest in developing fair-minded reasoning in the search for personal, social, and political transformation" (Weil, 1993, p. 211).

TERMINOLOGY The following concepts need to be considered when thinking about culture and diversity:

**Acculturation.**  This is the process by which the members of a society are taught the elements of that society's culture.  Everyone goes through an acculturation process, immigrants and non-immigrants alike.

**Common Culture.**  This refers to the common body of knowledge that allows diverse people to communicate, to work together, and to live together (Hirsch, 1993).

**Counter Culture.**  This refers to a protest movement in the late 1960s, in which young people formed their own culture in opposition of the culture of Middle America.  This movement was epitomized by "Hippies" and the Woodstock festival.

**Cultural Encapsulation.**  Similar to ethnocentrism, this is a closing-off of one culture from others.

**Cultural Literacy.**  This refers to the names, phrases, events, and other items that are familiar to most literate persons in a given culture (Hirsch, 1993).  To be culturally literate is to know the shared information that binds your culture together.

**Cultural Pluralism.**  This refers to the belief that diverse groups coexist within American society and maintain a culturally distinct identity.

**Cultural Understanding.**  This refers to the process of learning about other cultures in order to foster social harmony and growth.

**Ethnocentrism.**  This is the belief that one's cultural ways are not only valid and superior to other people's, but also universally applicable in evaluating and judging human behavior.

**Heritage.**  This refers to something that belongs to a person by reason of his or her birth.  A person may be born into one culture and later ignore or reject that cultural inheritance in favor of another.

**Intercultural.**  This means "between" or "among" cultures.  Intercultural interactions involve mutual or reciprocal exchanges.

**Melting Pot.** This refers to the concept that many cultures can blend into one. This concept has historically been a component of American culture. However, it no longer is widely accepted as a goal within our society.

**Microculture.** This implies a greater linkage with the larger culture, and emphasis is often put on the degree to which the microculture acts to interpret, express, and/or mediate the ideas, values, and institutions of the political community.

**Multicultural.** This refers to a number of diverse traditions, customs, arts, languages, values, and beliefs existing side-by-side.

**Subculture.** This is a term used frequently by sociologists to refer to a social group that shares characteristics that distinguish it in some way from the larger political society (usually called macro-culture) of which it is a part.

**Youth Culture.** Leisure, lifestyles, clothing styles, musical tastes, and peer-group values typically define youth cultures. Youth cultures exhibit particular rules of behavior which are often considered as deviant or in opposition to the dominant group.

Here are some tips to help improve your interactions in daily life, making you a better role model for your students.

❧ *Look at a dollar bill.* There is a slogan on our currency, written in Latin: "E pluribus unum." It means "From many, one," or "Wholeness incorporating diversity." Look at this phrase every time you exchange money with someone, whether it be a friend, a store clerk, a bank teller, or a starving person. If you find yourself feeling uncomfortable due to someone's cultural differences, give a dollar bill to that person and explain the meaning of the Latin slogan.

❧ *Cheerfully acknowledge differences.* Equality is not the product of similarity. Rather, it is the cheerful acknowledgment of difference (Cleveland, 1994). We are all equal in that we are equally different!

❧ *Identify the common culture.* When you meet someone of a different culture, try to identify the shared knowledge that allows the two of you to communicate, to work or play together, and to live together.

❧ *Identify differences within your own culture.* Within every cultural subgroup is a vast array of diversity. Before you quickly lump yourself or someone else into a cultural category, remember the number of differences which exist in every group. It is differences which foster growth, add richness, and make a culture dynamic.

🍃 *Stop stereotypical jokes.* When friends or relatives tell stereotypical jokes, they are exhibiting uncritical, narrow-minded thinking. Explain why you find that brand of humor offensive. Be a good example yourself by never lumping individual people into broad categories or making fun of others based upon stereotypes.

CLASSROOM
STRATEGIES

The following classroom strategies will prove useful in creating a classroom which fosters cultural understanding.

🍃 Create a safe environment, where all students feel respected and welcome (Pikulski and Cooper, 1996). Putting up posters which focus on diverse cultures is one way to send out the message that "all cultures are welcome here."

🍃 As you teach, briefly look individual students in the eye. This helps them recognize that you see and value them, and that you are teaching them as individuals, not just as "the class" (Lippy, 1996).

🍃 As you teach, mentally note your use of general pronouns. Use the pronouns "you" and "your" rather than "us," "we," and "our." "We" might suggest "everyone but you" to the student, while the personal "you" signals that you are speaking to each individual (Lippy, 1996).

🍃 Allow students to respond in ways that reflect their cultural diversity by using questioning techniques which personally involve them (Pikulski and Cooper, 1996).

🍃 Help to overcome stereotypes by engaging the students in role-playing exercises which encourage them to "trade places" with others and to express and examine their attitudes, beliefs, and feelings about such issues as prejudice and discrimination (Pikulski and Cooper, 1996).

🍃 Open discussions about literature encourage discussion of personal experiences and attitudes and open them for examination in a neutral way (Pikulski and Cooper, 1996).

🍃 Take advantage of cooperative learning which allows the group to benefit from individual strengths and styles, as each student brings his or her knowledge and experience to a project or task.

🍃 Have students research their family origins by creating a family tree and involve the whole class in exploring the differences.

- Recognize and celebrate the diversity in your community, your school, and your classroom by celebrating various holidays throughout the school year.

- Spotlight heroes of various nations and cultures with class projects and individual assignments. Emphasize cross-cultural research.

- Post the "Creed for Citizens of a Diverse World" (Griessman, 1993) on a bulletin board and share it with your class:

---

### Creed for Citizens of a Diverse World

*I believe that diversity is a part of the natural order of things— as natural as the trillion shapes and shades of the flowers of spring or the leaves of autumn. I believe that diversity brings new solutions to an ever-changing environment, and that sameness is not only uninteresting but limiting. To deny diversity is to deny life—with all its richness and manifold opportunities. Thus I affirm my citizenship in a world of diversity, and with it the responsibility to:*

**Be tolerant.** *Live and let live. Understand that those who cause no harm should not be feared, ridiculed, or harmed-even if they are different.*

**Look** *for the best in others.*

**Be just** *in my dealing with poor and rich, weak and strong, and whenever possible, to defend the young, the old, the frail, the defenseless.*

**Avoid** *needless conflicts and diversions, but always be willing to change for the better that which can be changed.*

**Seek** *knowledge in order to know what can be changed, as well as, what cannot be changed.*

**Forge** *alliances with others who love liberty and justice.*

**Be kind,** *remembering how fragile the human spirit is.*

**Be generous** *in thought, word, and purse.*

**Live** *the examined life, subjecting my motives and actions to the scrutiny of mind and heart so to rise above prejudice and hatred.*

**Care.**

---

Finally, let's look again at the opening scenario. Read the situation below and record your reactions. The process of answering the questions will help you to prepare for handling cultural diversity in your classroom. There is no one "right" answer, so be thoughtful and be yourself.

Setting: The school cafeteria at lunch time. You have lunch duty and are eating at a table near the students.

Time: The period has just begun; some students are still finding seats as they come through the food line.

Person involved: A new student, Billy, and two of your best students, Bryan and José.

Background: Billy has transferred from a small, rural town in the South. Bryan and José are among the best students in the class and are the most popular boys.

Circumstances: Your school is located in a large, urban Northeastern area of the country.

Simulation: Bryan and José respond with obvious dislike to the new student, Billy, shutting him out of their group and marking him as "unacceptable" to the entire class with their rejection and mimicing of him. Bryan says, "I can't stand that brown-noser. All he does is suck up to the teachers." "Yeah," José replies, imitating Billy's voice, "Yes, Ma'am; no, Ma'am; excuse me, Sir!" Their ridicule carries a great deal of weight with their classmates, and you realize that Billy's chances for social adjustment are poor without their help.

1. What is your objective?

_____

_____

_____

2. Do you turn and address the students in the lunch room? If no, why? If yes, what do you say?

_____

_____

_____

3. Do you talk to Billy about the differences between the culture of the rural South and the urban Northeast? If so, what advice would you give him? If not, why not?

_____

_____

_____

4. If you were to attempt to describe a situation in your own life where cultural differences made you uncomfortable about yourself or another, what example would you give?

_____

_____

_____

_____

CONCLUSION

Our world is like a shimmering diamond, every facet representing a unique culture. It is virtually impossible to escape the influence of culture, no matter what you do or where you go. When rivers meet, they flow, but cultures often just collide. In the calming of the collision, we can all be heard more clearly stating who we are (Center for Cultural Interchange, 1996). Intercultural communication skills are a necessity for everyone, not just for the culturally "deprived" or distinct, but for all people as cultural beings.

Diversity enriches the lives of individuals and strengthens society as a whole. Diversity expands the possibilities for progress, evolution, and positive change in the world because it allows us to see from many different perspectives. If human beings were free of differences, the quality of our lives would be profoundly diminished.

Multicultural education honors individuality while promoting respect for all members of our society regardless of ethnicity, gender, religion, race, or sexual orientation, and thus teaches children how to be effective members of a democracy. It emphasizes understanding rather than rote learning and has as its goal a change in the learner as a result of that new understanding (Covert, 1996).

REFERENCES    Arvizu, S. R., Snyder, W. A., & Espinosa, P. T. (1980, June). Demystifying the concept of culture: Theoretical and conceptual tools. *Bilingual Education Paper Series*, *3*(11). Los Angeles: Evaluation, Dissemination and Assessment Center, California State University, Los Angeles.

Bienvenu, M. J. & Colonomos, B. (1993). *An introduction to deaf culture: Rules of social interaction.* Burtonsville, MD: Sign Media.

Center for Cultural Interchange. (1996). *Host family handbook.* St. Charles, IL: Author.

Cleveland, H. (1994). The limits of cultural diversity. *Vital Speeches*, *60*, 756.

Covert, P. (1996). Some initial thoughts on multicultural education. In *Multicultural Pavilion* [On-line]. Available: http:// teis.virginia.edu/curry/centers/multicultural/initial.html#principles

Gordon, E. & Roberts, F. (1991). *Report of social studies syllabus review and development committee.* Albany: The State Education Department and the University of the State of New York.

Greissman, B. E. (1992). *Diversity challenges and opportunities.* New York: Harper Collins.

Hirsch, E. D. (1993). *The dictionary of cultural literacy.* Boston: Houghton Mifflin Co.

James, J. (1995). Cultural diversity in the classrooms. In *Teacher Talk* [On-line]. Available: http://educ/indiana.edu/cas/tt/v2i2/ cultural.html

Lippy, E. (1996). Teaching tip of the week. In *Teacher's Corner* [On-line]. Available: http://berean.org/cef_docs/tt960422.htm

Pikulski, J. J. & Cooper, J. D. (1996). Issues in literacy development. In *Education Place* [On-line]. Available: http:// www.hmco.com/hmco/school/rdg/res/literacy/multi2.html

Rorty, A. O. (1995). Rights: Educational, not cultural. *Social Research*, *62*, 161.

Weil, D. (1993). Towards a critical multicultural literacy: Advancing an education for liberation. *Roeper Review*, *15*, 211.

# Race and Ethnicity in the Classroom

OBJECTIVES

By the end of this chapter, you should be able to answer these questions:

❦ What is the classroom teacher's biggest challenge in terms of race?
❦ How are the concepts of race and ethnicity distinguished?
❦ What is the United States Census Bureau's definition of race?
❦ What is the difference between scapegoating and discrimination?
❦ What are two factors responsible for blurring racial distinctions?

THE CLASSROOM IS A MICROCOSM

*It is a few minutes before the first class of the day. Two girls enter your classroom early, chatting as they take their seats. You are doing some last minute planning at your desk. As you look up to greet them you hear the first girl, Sue, say to the second girl, Mary, "I don't like him. He's black, and anyway my dad says blacks shouldn't be in this school because they just cause trouble." You are aware that Mary's father is African-American, though Mary has Caucasian features and coloring. Mary does not respond to her friend, but looks downcast and turns away, changing the subject.*

INTRODUCTION

Race is a controversial and explosive category of human diversity. Currently there is a political and social trend toward minimizing racial differences and emphasizing human similarities. According to some anthropologists, there is no such thing as race at all. However, interracial tensions and hostilities persist, and many people feel that by minimizing differences we risk losing valuable racial and ethnic distinctions which we should celebrate.

There are few places where a greater probability exists of encountering racial and ethnic diversity than in the classroom. As a teacher, you will be challenged to create harmony from many different voices as you teach respect for diversity while stressing our common human attributes. You will have the task of examining your own attitudes and prejudices as well as those of your students as you cultivate fair and objective attitudes.

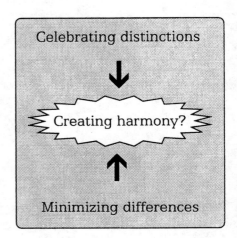

Celebrating distinctions
⬇
Creating harmony?
⬆
Minimizing differences

A good first step in preparing to deal with racial and ethnic diversity in the classroom is the following self-test. It will help you to assess your own thoughts and feelings about these issues. We have accumulated concepts and attitudes throughout our lives, some of which we may never have consciously examined.

---

### Are You a Racist?

*Circle yes or no for each of the following:*

1. Y / N    Do you believe that your country would have fewer racial problems if different people would keep to their own kind?
2. Y / N    Would it bother you to learn after an accident that you received a blood transfusion from someone of a different race?
3. Y / N    Have you ever invited a person of another race into your home for a social occasion?
4. Y / N    Would your friends be understanding if you married a person of another race?
5. Y / N    Do you believe that some races are naturally superior to others?
6. Y / N    Would you be reluctant to adopt a child of a different race?
7. Y / N    Do you think that people of some races are more intelligent than others?
8. Y / N    Do you think people of some races are more hard-working than others?
9. Y / N    Do you think legal immigrants are stealing American jobs?
10. Y / N    Would you send your child to a private school that did not accept racially diverse students?
11. Y / N    Do you feel uncomfortable around people of different races?
12. Y / N    Does it make you uneasy to see a man holding hands with a woman of a different race?
13. Y / N    Do you have any racially diverse friends?
14. Y / N    Do you believe that so-called minorities are poor because they fail to take advantage of the opportunities open to them?

[Adapted from Patterson, J. & Kim, P. (1991). *The day America told the truth.* New York: Plume.]

---

Now turn the page to determine your score.

Give yourself one point each if you answered "yes" to questions 1, 2, 5, 6, 7, 8, 9, 10, 11, 12, 14. Give yourself one point each if you answered "no" to questions 3, 4, 13.

How did you score?

9 - 14 = *stubborn racist*—you categorize and judge people based solely upon race.

7 - 8 = *bigoted*—you are generally intolerant of any race that is not your own.

5 - 6 = *prejudiced*—you have preconceived ideas about people based upon race.

3 - 4 = *biased*—your personal preferences color some of your judgments.

2 = *tolerant*—you grant others their rights but still see differences based upon race.

0 - 1 = *color-blind*—you do not categorize or judge people based upon race.

Few people are totally color-blind. Even if you scored zero on the racism scale, it's crucial to learn more about race in order to more effectively combat racism in the classroom.

PERSPECTIVE
ONE

Much of what we think of as racial culture is really geographic and social in nature. When we speak about diversity we are often talking about different cultures more than different races, though racial difference may be superficially apparent in facial features and skin pigmentation.

In a typical classroom in the United States you may have students from many different places in the world, and it is important to remember that race is distinct from country of origin. What would you expect to be the geographic origin of a student whose skin is black?

_____

What about a student who has Oriental features?

_____

What about a student who has light brown skin?

_____

Be careful not to draw hasty conclusions. Consider the fact that children of African origin, for instance, may be of any race, and "African culture" is different in different parts of the world. For example, people in the Congo share a cultural heritage with the French, Somalians are culturally defined by their Muslim heritage, and the African American population has created its own unique culture influenced by America's diverse immigrant population. What are some reasons why race is not necessarily linked to culture?

_____

_____

_____

Immigration and world travel have increased exponentially in the past several decades, blurring distinctions of race and culture. This cultural change is reflected in the classroom, and to be a successful teacher of a diverse student population you must be aware of its complexity. Why do you think it is imperative for a classroom teacher to understand cultural differences?

_____

_____

_____

_____

Children learn values and social behavior from their families and their social groups. These values and behaviors are carried over into attitudes toward authority, social interactions with peers, and approaches to learning.

PERSPECTIVE
TWO

Unlike race, ethnicity can definitely be linked to culture. Ethnicity refers to how members of a group perceive themselves and how they are in turn perceived by others. *Ethnic* describes a group of people within a larger society that is socially distinguished or set apart by others and/or itself, primarily on the

*VOICES OF EXPERIENCE*

*"I want to let you know what it's like being a black teacher in a predominantly white school. I come from the island of St. Martin and was raised speaking British English, so my students find my choice of words sometimes funny and they like to correct me. Since the purpose of class is to learn, I look at it as a chance for students to teach me as well. I teach them chemistry, and they teach me how to pronounce 'picture' correctly. Sometimes it is a revelation for them to find out that things are correct even if it is not the 'normal' way of saying them. For example, I say the plural of fish is fishes; they say it is fish. We looked it up in a dictionary and found out that we were both right, even though my way was different. We learn from each other."*
*—Marsha Ritter-Jones, teacher (1995, p. 2)*

basis of cultural characteristics. What are some typical characteristics that distinguish such groups?

_____

_____

Ethnic groups may share a language, religion, nationality, or history which draws them together and gives them a common identity. Just as with race, however, ethnic distinctions may be blurred. For example, you may have students whose parents each come from different ethnic cultures. A child with a Catholic, Cuban mother and a German, Protestant father may identify with any or all of the ethnic and cultural groups which a rich family heritage offers.

So the challenge for the classroom teacher is to focus on *human* attributes, while keeping aware of and honoring ethnic differences. Educators need an understanding of how students are actually prevented from building bridges over ethnic and racial boundaries, not only within a school setting but also with peers who are different from themselves (Garcia 1994, p. 185). Name one possible "boundary" that might make it difficult for students to connect with each other.

_____

_____

A typical boundary occurs when one ethnic group perceives another as not being equal. In other words, one group values certain qualities in the other more highly than in its own. Psychologists suggest that members of ethnic groups "may pay particular attention to differences between themselves and others in order to bolster a positive sense of their social identity" (Bower 1996, p. 409). Therefore, individuals in two different groups may be prevented from connecting with each other on "neutral ground" (Garcia 1994, p. 184).

Clearly, ethnic identity is closely tied to a student's self-concept. The classroom teacher cannot be expected to untie such a complicated and deeply-rooted knot, nor would doing so necessarily be appropriate. However, there are strategies for helping students to loosen that knot themselves. One such strategy would be to help students distinguish between human attributes and ethnic differences. Human attributes are universal—all humans have skin, all humans have feelings, all humans get thirsty, and so on. Ethnic differences are particular—some people celebrate Cinco de Mayo, some people observe Rosh Hashanah, some people square dance, and so on. List some qualities which you consider

to be universal by completing the following sentence:
*Regardless of their apparent differences, all human beings...*

_____

_____

The typical classroom in the United States today will have a racially diverse population. As we noted earlier in this chapter, racial makeup may or may not be apparent and should never be confused with place of origin or with ethnic identity. What is the source or derivation of racial difference?

_____

_____

_____

Racial differentiation is a result of evolution and genetic mixing, and human races vary greatly around the world. List all the different races you are aware of:

_____

_____

_____

_____

We see many races in America because of our large immigrant population, but we are most familiar with only a few of the larger racial categories. Therefore, there is a danger of "lumping" students into such broad groups as "African," "Asian," "Native American," or "Hispanic."

Remember that, as Edward Babun (1969) pointed out in *The Varieties of Man*, people of genetically diverse

> ## Spotlight
> ### on the Classroom
>
> "My son is adopted. We brought him to the United States from Korea in 1980. When he was old enough, we talked to him about the fact that he was born in another country but that now he was American.
>
> "Shortly after he started kindergarten, he began to resist going to school. When we questioned him, he said that the children called him names because he is Chinese.
>
> "'But that's silly,' we told him. 'You're not Chinese, you're Korean.' What he said made me realize that I had no way to help him understand racism, because I couldn't understand it myself.
>
> "'But Mom,' he said, 'they don't know any names for Koreans, so that's why they call me a Chink.'
>
> "He had already accepted the idea that racism was a given, and he was only 5 years old."
> —Dinah L., parent

populations look different only superficially. Describe some of these physical differences:

_____

_____

_____

_____

Skin color, facial features, body build, and hair type are differences which are apparent to us. Less obvious differences may be such things as susceptibility to various diseases, tolerance of extreme temperatures, frequencies of blood type, or other aspects of biochemistry and physiology. In spite of all these differences, human races make up one species, *Homo sapiens* (Babun, 1969).

In the gene pool of any given race is an astronomical number of possible chromosome combinations. Differences among races account for a mere six percent of human genetic variation. Differences among tribes or nations within a race account for only eight percent of variation. Individual variation within local groups, on the other hand, accounts for eighty-five percent of genetic difference (Myers, 1995). Therefore, the average genetic difference between two Siberians or two Cubans is much greater than the difference between the two groups. Not all Japanese people are short with black hair. Not all Norwegians are tall with blond hair. In every race, the range of difference is vast.

It will often happen that your students will have backgrounds in two or more races, making it difficult for you to classify them in that way. According to the United States Census Bureau, in fact, race now reflects self-description rather than denoting any scientific test of biological inheritance. How a student defines his or her race will often depend upon which one he or she most closely identifies with (Famighetti, 1993). Do you identify with only one race, or with more than one? Which one(s)?

_____

What factors do you use to separate yourself into a particular race?

_____

_____

Skin color is the most common factor people use for racial classification. However, skin color is the perfect example of how race is relative. Depending upon what society or circumstance you are in, the shade of your skin may be variously interpreted. For example, the Creoles of Louisiana, a French-speaking people of mixed racial heritage, are variously seen as black, white, or Creole, depending upon the context (Auerbach, 1994).

The problem with racial classification goes deeper than merely what categories or how many categories we choose to use. Geneticists have had trouble even identifying the gene or sets of genes responsible for race, and many now claim that race does not exist.

The idea of race is actually relatively new in human history. The term was coined by the French naturalist George Louis Leclerc Buffon in 1749. Perhaps the concept could disappear just as quickly as it was invented. "If members of society refused to believe that skin color and certain other physical traits were important, the concept of race would not exist" (Auerbach, 1994, p. 1377).

TERMINOLOGY

Following is a list of terms which you should be able to define and to distinguish between:

**Americanization.** A synonym for the "melting pot" phenomenon, this term refers to a practice of acculturation that seeks to merge small ethnic and linguistically diverse communities into a single dominant national culture (Garcia, 1994).

**Bias.** This is a personal preference which prevents one from making fair judgments or assessments.

**Bigotry.** This is a stubborn intolerance of any race, nationality, or creed that differs from one's own.

**Discrimination.** This is differential treatment based on unfair categorization. Acting on prejudice results in discrimination. Discrimination often involves isolating people from places or activities based upon the groups to which they belong.

**Ethnicity.** This arises from the cultural commodities that are shared by a number of individuals (Auerbach, 1994). Such commodities are magnets that draw individuals together, providing them with a group identity and consciousness. The beliefs of individuals about their own ethnic group tend to be similar to, and more positive than, the beliefs of those outside the group.

**Minority.** Although this term should simply be used to describe a subset within a population, it often connotes inferior status in comparison to the majority. Often the minority is a sociological term referring to a social group that occupies a subordinate position in a society.

**Nationality.** This simply refers to the country where a person was born. Nationality is not necessarily linked to a person's culture, ethnicity, or race.

**Prejudice.** Literally meaning to "pre-judge," this is an unsupported opinion accompanied by rigid disapproval. Prejudice is learned, not innate.

**Race.** This is an anthropological concept used to divide humankind into categories based on physical characteristics such as size and shape of the head, eyes, ears, lips, and nose, and the color of skin and eyes (Bennett, 1993). Race has never been scientifically equated with any mental characteristics such as intelligence, personality, or character.

**Racism.** This is the belief that one race is superior to another based on the erroneous assumption that physical attributes of a group determine their psychological, social, or intellectual characteristics (Bennett, 1986).

**Scapegoating.** This refers to the deliberate blaming of an individual or group when the fault lies elsewhere. Prejudicial attitudes and discriminatory acts often lead to scapegoating, which can result in verbal and physical violence, including death.

**Stereotyping.** This is a preconceived or oversimplified generalization involving beliefs about a particular group. Negative stereotypes are often the basis for prejudice. Stereotyping ignores individuals and instead categorizes them as members of a group who all think and act alike. We may learn stereotypes from what others say, from books and movies, and from subtle cues we observe in society in general.

**Tolerance.** This is the opposite of bigotry. Tolerance refers to a fair and objective attitude toward races, nationalities, and practices different from one's own. However, tolerance implies disapproval. Tolerance does not celebrate diversity but merely puts up with it.

Here are some slogans to share with students, designed to help them to empower themselves against racist attitudes and behaviors:

🍎 I am a member of the *human* race.

🍎 I can take a stand against racist behavior.

🍎 I can remove "race" from my vocabulary.

🍎 I can practice looking at people and not labels.

🍎 I can treat everyone I meet as an equal.

🍎 I can take differences at "face value."

🍎 I can celebrate a particular ethnic culture.

The following classroom strategies (adapted from Bosworth, 1995) are designed to help teachers work with student populations comprised of many racial and ethnic groups. Clearly, these strategies are appropriate for any student population, whether racially mixed or not. A good rule of thumb is to approach every classroom as if it were racially mixed, incorporating multiculturalism into the curriculum whenever possible.

🍎 Check textbooks and other materials for multiracial representations. Does the book show pictures only of people with light skin?

🍎 Mix students in groups. In the cooperative learning technique, students are given an assignment to complete as a group, thereby fostering cooperation across racial/ethnic lines.

🍎 Inform parents about what is happening in your classroom. As an additional reinforcement, encourage the class to develop a monthly newsletter about various class activities to be disseminated to parents.

🍎 Avoid biased expectations based upon race or ethnicity. Develop a questionnaire about current biases and stereotypes and allow students to complete it anonymously. Read the responses aloud and let the class as a whole discuss the validity or non-validity of each item.

🍎 Encourage students to attend ethnic events and to share their experiences with the class. Arranging field trips throughout the year is an excellent way to facilitate this activity for those students who may not have support outside of school.

🍎 Teach students appropriate ways of discussing race and ethnicity, including correct terminology. Disallow inappropriate slang to be used during discussions.

Finally, let's return to the scenario that opened this chapter. Read the situation below and record your reactions. Answering the questions will prepare you to handle diversity in the classroom. Remember that there is no one "right" answer.

Setting: Homeroom

Time: A few minutes before class starts

Persons involved: Sue, of Caucasian ancestry, and Mary, of African American ancestry but with Caucasian features

Background: You are aware that Mary's father is African American; her classmates assume she is Caucasian

Circumstances: You are working at your desk. The two girls enter the room early, chatting as they take their seats.

Simulation: Sue says to Mary, "I don't like him. He's black, and anyway my dad says blacks shouldn't be in this school because they just cause trouble." Mary does not respond to her friend, but looks downcast and turns away, changing the subject.

1. What are you going to do?

_____

_____

_____

2. What are your objectives?

_____

_____

_____

3. What are your options?

_____

_____

_____

_____

4. Will you talk to Sue privately? If yes, what will you say? If no, why?

_____

_____

_____

5. Will you talk to Mary privately? If yes, what will you say? If no, why?

_____

_____

_____

6. What can you do to help prevent such situations in the future?

_____

_____

_____

CONCLUSION

By now you may be thinking, "All this is well and good, and I am ready to work on being color blind, but categorizing by race is required in many contexts." You would be correct. We use racial labels on birth certificates, marriage licenses, college applications, school enrollment and health forms, and many other official documents. We use race to determine eligibility for scholarships and grants, and sometimes for admission into a school or special program. We are clearly caught in the middle of a paradigm shift, where our conception of what "race" means is changing.

We must also change our idea of what "minority" means. In 1995, nearly one in every four Americans was a member of a so-called minority racial or ethnic group, and the Bureau of Census estimates that by the year 2050, the percentage of the population that is White (not Hispanic) will decrease from 75.7 percent (in 1990) to 52.7 percent (Landes, 1994). So, as you can see, the word "minority" is quickly losing its meaning as "a smaller part" as well as its connotation of something less than the majority. We are in the process of refining and redefining what we mean when we use racial categories. The very fact that we are examining our old ideas offers hope of a more enlightened attitude.

REFERENCES        Auerbach, S. (Ed.). (1994). *The encyclopedia of multiculturalism.* (Vol. 5). New York: Marshall Cavendish.

Babun, E. (1969). *The varieties of man: An introduction to human races.* London: Collier-Macmillan.

Bennett, C. E. (1993). The black population in the United States. *Current Population Reports*, 20-471.

Bennett, C. I. (1986). *Comprehensive multicultural education: Theory and practice.* Boston: Allyn and Bacon.

Bosworth, K. (1995). Cultural diversity in the classrooms. In *Teacher Talk* [On-line]. Available: http://educ/indiana.edu/cas/tt/v2i2/cultural.html

Bower, B. (1996, June 29). Fighting stereotype stigma: Studies chart accuracy, usefulness of inferences about social groups. *Science News, 149,* 408-409.

Famighetti, R. (Ed.). (1993). *The world almanac and book of facts 1994.* Mahwah, NJ: Funk and Wagnalls.

Garcia, E. (1994). *Understanding and meeting the challenge of student cultural diversity.* Boston: Houghton Mifflin.

Jones, M. R. (1995). When the teacher is a minority. In *Teacher Talk* [On-line]. Available: http://educ/indiana.edu/cas/tt/v2i2/when.html

Landes, A. (Ed.). (1994). *Minorities: A changing role in America.* Wylie, TX: Information Plus.

Myers, D. G. (1995). *Psychology.* New York: Hope.

Patterson, J. & Kim, P. (1991). *The day America told the truth.* New York: Plume.

# Sexual Identity in the Classroom

**4**

OBJECTIVES

By the end of this chapter you should be able to answer these questions:

- What is the difference between sex and gender?
- What is the best way to respond to sexist biases and stereotypes?
- What labels are appropriate for describing sexual orientation?
- When is teacher intervention appropriate in matters of a student's sexual identity or gender discrimination?

THE CLASSROOM IS A MICROCOSM

*After weeks of preparation, rehearsals, and anticipation, the costumes for the school play have arrived. You pass out individual packages to each of your students, and a few minutes of animated talking ensue as everyone examines and compares outfits. Then you hear Tom, one of the lead actors in the play, loudly announce that he will not participate. "There's no way I'm wearing these panty hose," he exclaims, holding up a pair of black tights. "I'm not dressing like some queer!" The rest of the students suddenly go into an uproar.*

INTRODUCTION

From the moment of birth, when the doctor says, "It's a boy" or "It's a girl," our parents, peers, and society begin to shape our sexual identity. Prejudice based upon gender and sexual orientation potentially affects every human being, because each of us has gender and sexual orientation. As Schuman and Olufs (1995) have pointed out, it is important to remember that gender is not the same as sex. Sex is a biological classification, relating to specific organs of reproduction. Gender is a much broader topic which focuses on the roles occupied by males and females.

There is a question as to whether sex and gender are even related, and so we use the word *gender* to make the distinction (Schuman & Olufs, 1995).

Why do you suppose it is so difficult for most of us to address issues

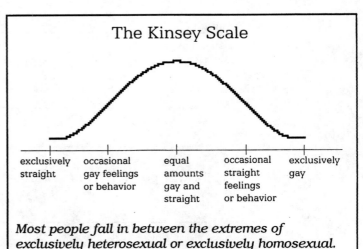

The Kinsey Scale

exclusively straight | occasional gay feelings or behavior | equal amounts gay and straight | occasional straight feelings or behavior | exclusively gay

*Most people fall in between the extremes of exclusively heterosexual or exclusively homosexual.*

of gender and sexuality?

_____

_____

Our sexuality is so fundamentally a part of who we are that it is a most difficult subject to discuss objectively. There are differing scientific views about gender differences and about the definition and roots of sexual orientation. However, everyone agrees on one point: the issues are complex and few people can address them without emotion. That is probably because we are all sexual beings, and therefore the subject is very personal. It is also laden with myriad religious, cultural, and social inhibitions, taboos, and rules.

**VOICES OF EXPERIENCE**

*"We hold these truths to be self-evident, that all men and women are created equal."*
—*First Women's Rights Convention, July 19, 1848*

So many biases based on gender and sexual orientation are built into our laws and systems of education that we may be unaware of how deeply they affect us and our children. An interesting way to begin thinking about how integral these biases are is to take the following test (Adapted from Bass and Kaufman, 1996, pp. 252-253) which was designed to assist heterosexuals in thinking about homosexuality. We realize that this test is only appropriate for approximately 90% of our readers.

**Sexual Orientation Questionnaire**

1. What do you think caused your heterosexuality?

_____

_____

2. When and how did you first decide you were heterosexual?

_____

_____

3. Is it possible your heterosexuality is just a phase you might outgrow?

_____

_____

4. Is it possible that your heterosexuality stems from a neurotic fear of others of the same sex?

_____

_____

5. What compels heterosexuals to seduce others into their lifestyle?

_____

_____

6. Why do heterosexuals insist on flaunting their heterosexuality?  Why can't they just be what they are, and keep it quiet?

_____

_____

7. Would you want your children to be heterosexual, knowing the problems they would face?

_____

_____

8. Since almost all child molesters are heterosexual, do you consider it safe to expose your children to heterosexual teachers?

_____

_____

9. Even with all the societal support marriage receives, there is a 50% divorce rate.  Why are there so few stable heterosexual relationships?

_____

_____

10. Why do heterosexuals place so much emphasis on sex?

_____

_____

Whether children are male or female, the way their gender is perceived and treated in the world is of great importance. It is also of great importance how teachers perceive themselves individually and in society, because that perception affects the lessons they impart to their students—consciously or unconsciously—about gender and sexual orientation. Though both men and women in the United States enjoy more freedom than people in much of the rest of the world, the struggle for gender equity is ongoing.

What societal problems regarding sexual orientation and gender are you aware of?

> **VOICES OF EXPERIENCE**
>
> *"Sugar and spice and all things nice,
> And such are little girls made of.
> Snips and snails and puppy dog tails,
> And such are little boys made of."*
> —Robert Southey, poet
>
> *"A little girl is treated and molded differently from a little boy from the day she is born."*
> —Dr. Benjamin Spock, pediatrician and educator

_____

_____

_____

Sexual harassment, sexist institutions, gay bashing, and domestic violence continue to thwart the fight for equal rights, to affect our children, and to spill over as crucial issues into the classrooms of the United States.

The following negative statements reflect some common stereotypes that prevail in our society. How would you respond to the following student statements?

"Women can't be fire fighters. They're too weak and sometimes too emotional."

_____

_____

"Homosexuals shouldn't be allowed to adopt or have custody of children."

_____

_____

"Men are the perpetrators, not the victims, of sexual harassment."

_____

_____

"If people are married or have children, they must be heterosexual."

_____

_____

Whenever you hear negative statements such as those listed above, it may prove useful to note that stereotypes can be false. Since we know that both men and women—regardless of gender or sexual orientation—have served bravely in the military, have successfully parented children, taught school, and succeeded in virtually all professions, it would seem pointless to question anyone's orientation or to judge someone based upon gender.

Gender equity is a complex problem in the classroom and in the world at large. Let's look for a moment at some issues regarding traditional male roles. How would you finish the following sentence?

"We live in a _____ dominated society."

We have all heard, and generally accepted, that we live in a male-dominated society, but it is important not to overlook some important and disturbing facts about what it is like to be a male. While a small minority of men may indeed still hold most of the power in our world, the majority of males are suffering from the deterioration of their traditional roles. Statistics on male addiction, suicide, and depression are alarming. Consider the following (derived from Myers, 1995):

- Male teenagers are five times more likely to take their own lives than females.
- Overall, males commit suicide at four times the rate of females.
- Males between the ages of 18 and 29 suffer alcohol dependency at three times the rate of females of the same age group.
- More than two-thirds of all alcoholics are males.
- Males account for more than 90 percent of arrests for alcohol and drug abuse violations.
- Sixty percent of all high school dropouts are males.

In many communities—especially those in the inner cities—men are often absent from the home as well as from the schools. Do you see the importance of men becoming more involved in education?  If so, why?  If not, why not?

_____

_____

_____

Education must have as a primary goal the reestablishment of a male voice in our schools.  We must provide men with greater opportunities to be teachers and role models in early-grade classes, where their presence can help fatherless boys to develop self-esteem and give girls positive images of males.  We can also show concern for our communities by encouraging the participation of both men and women in community-based boys' and girls' clubs, scout troops, sports leagues, religious organizations, and big brother and big sister programs.

PERSPECTIVE
Two

We are born with our gender, but where does our sexual orientation come from?  Do we choose it?  What do you think?

_____

_____

_____

Our sexual orientation is an invisible quality.  Scientists disagree about whether we choose our orientation, are led to it by our environment and social interactions, or are born with it.  Many experts now believe it is a combination of factors.

Suppose there are twenty children in your class, some male and some female.  How many would you expect are not heterosexual?

_____

It's likely that two or more of your students will not be heterosexual. Estimates of the incidence of homosexuality vary depending upon how strictly homosexuality is defined and the methodology of the study.  The Kinsey Report of 1948 estimated that ten percent of the adult population was homosexual, and most current estimates tend to lean toward the ten-percent level.  However, a University of Chicago survey in 1994— where researchers who were strangers to the respondents asked questions regarding sexual orientation—put the number at about three percent (Gallagher, 1994).  Such low figures need to be considered carefully due to the methods utilized in the study. What might be some reasons for the seeming discrepancies in these studies?

_____

_____

_____

Due to social stigmas and people's reluctance to confide private information to a relative stranger, any statistic on sexuality must be taken with a grain of salt.

PERSPECTIVE
THREE We all necessarily use labels to describe specific actions and attributes, but labeling sexual orientation poses special problems in the classroom. Name some specific reasons for the difficulty posed by this issue of labeling:

_____

_____

_____

It is problematic even for doctors and mental health professionals to find appropriate and accurate labels for sexual orientation. The subject is too complex, and human feelings, thoughts, and actions are seldom easy to objectify. Children and adolescents are developing and struggling with their sexual identities and are especially vulnerable to assault on their self-esteem.

We cannot use the term *sexual orientation* to divide people into two groups, heterosexual and homosexual. Sexuality is not black or white. Rather, many people fall into some category between the two extremes. It is important to note that sexual behavior and sexual orientation are not the same. Some people who engage in sexual activity with same sex partners do not consider themselves gay or lesbian. Author Gore Vidal once suggested that there is no such thing as a homosexual or heterosexual *person*—there are only homosexual and heterosexual *activities*. We use the terms *gay* (men), *lesbian* (women), or *homosexual* to describe people who participate in sexual activity with persons of their same sex. We use *heterosexual* or *straight* to describe those who participate in sexual activity with the opposite sex. *Bisexual* refers to men and women who may participate in sexual activity with both genders.

The majority of human beings describe themselves as heterosexual. Does that mean that only they are normal?

---

Virtually all experts on human psychology agree that within everyone there exists both feminine and masculine traits. There is no "normal" or "abnormal" orientation, and homosexuality is not a disease (Reiss, 1980). Both aggression and sensitivity can be found in every emotionally healthy person, regardless of gender.

PERSPECTIVE FOUR

Our society makes many assumptions about what and how males and females should be, as Maria Ekstrand (1995) notes. Gender stereotyping refers to the idea that, depending upon your gender, you should look, dress, act, think, and even feel certain ways. It is the practice of dividing males and females into different groups, though gender may have nothing to do with how they really feel, think, or act (Ekstrand, 1995). Can you give some examples of these stereotypical divisions in school?

_____

_____

_____

_____

What percentage of male students take home economics? What percentage of girls take shop or auto mechanics? Are there classroom activities which you assume are "for boys" or "for girls"? Though there has been an attempt to break down these biases and divisions, we still have far to go.

Why is it so important to make changes in the way we perceive gender divisions?

_____

_____

_____

_____

As Shargel and Kane (1974) stated, children whose interests and activities are limited on the basis of gender are not making free choices. They will be able to discover who they are and what they want to become only when we not only allow but actively help them to unlearn the sexist and biased information they have taken in (Shargel and Kane, 1974).

Why is the teacher's role so vital in this "unlearning" process?

_____

_____

Other than parents, teachers are the central role models for children. If we can integrate change into our classrooms, as Shargel and Kane suggest, we can challenge the stereotypes of the wider society.

How and when do you think teachers should intervene?

_____

_____

_____

Shargel and Kane (1974) suggested teacher intervention to support children when their behavior or attitudes appear to challenge traditional roles or beliefs. Teachers should intervene whenever they notice that children are being constrained by gender stereotypes, or criticized by other children or adults for acting on their own interests and feelings. Teachers must take strong stands against harassment, slurs, and scapegoating, and guard consistently against the more subtle forms of stereotyping.

Perhaps a female student prefers playing football with the boys at recess over playing with the girls. Or perhaps a male student enjoys reading Nancy Drew mysteries. How can you intervene appropriately if you see students being penalized for their choices?

_____

_____

_____

You can strongly support their freedom to choose, making clear by your words and your example that you admire their courage in exercising their right to be different and pointing out exceptions to the stereotype in question.

TERMINOLOGY    Familiarize yourself with these important terms relating to gender and sexual orientation:

**Androgynous.** This refers to a person who exhibits masculine and feminine qualities, appearances, or behaviors.

**Asexualism.** A person who is asexual has no sexual feelings for either men or women.

**Bisexual.** This refers to people who participate in sexual activity with members of both genders.

**Chauvinism.** This is a prejudicial belief that one gender is superior to the other.

**Coming out.** This refers to the process of accepting one's own sexual orientation and telling others about it.

**Gay.** This is a term for males who participate in sexual activity with members of the same sex.

**Gender.** This is a term which refers to the different roles occupied by males and females.

**Heterosexism.** This refers to discrimination based upon the assumption that heterosexuality is the only viable or acceptable orientation.

**Heterosexual.** This refers to people who participate in sexual activity with members of the opposite sex.

**Homophobia.** This is a dislike or distrust stemming from feelings about a person's sexual orientation or lifestyle.

**Homosexual.** This refers to people who participate in sexual activity with members of the same sex.

**Lesbian.** This refers to females who participate in sexual activity with members of the same sex.

**Pedophilia.** This refers to adult men or women who seek sexual satisfaction from children. Pedophiles fall into neither heterosexual or homosexual categories. Though pedophiles are often erroneously thought to be homosexual, it is not the gender of the child that they are attracted to but rather the child's prepubescence.

**Sex.** This term is a biological classification and refers to one's reproductive organs.

**Sexism.** This refers to prejudice and discrimination against a particular gender.

**Sexual harassment.** This includes, but is not limited to, name-calling, innuendo, insults, obscene gestures, gay-bashing jokes, physical threats, and actual violence. Cutting classes and dropping out of school are two common ways students cope with sexual harassment they face at school (Bass and Kaufman, 1996).

**Straight.** This is a term for people who participate in sexual activity with members of the opposite sex.

**Transvestism.** This refers to a compulsion to wear the clothes of the other gender. Contrary to popular belief, male transvestites are predominantly heterosexual, not homosexual.

**Transsexualism.** This refers to individuals who have undergone or are in the process of undergoing a sex change operation because they are not comfortable with the gender with which they were born. Transsexualism is not related to sexual orientation, but rather has to do with physiology.

Following are some helpful guidelines that you can share with your students to foster their "unlearning" of gender biases and stereotypes:

- *Work to safeguard the basic rights of all people by supporting rules and laws which guarantee those rights.* On a daily basis, offer your help. Some students and fellow teachers may be uncomfortable with their own sexuality and may need your friendly support.

- *Be aware of the attitudes your students and co-workers are expressing.* Ask people not to tell sexist jokes or use sexist language.

- *Try to acknowledge when someone takes even small steps in the direction of tolerance and sensitivity.* Set an example by avoiding judging others. Refer only to your own behavior.

- *Don't assume that anyone or everyone is heterosexual.* Assume that you do not know anyone's sexual orientation for certain. Accordingly, do not use language that may be offensive.

- *Avoid biased speech and writing.* We can help to remove bias in our speech and in writing by using terms such as "same-gender," "male-male," "female-female," and "male-female" sexual behavior when referring to sexual pairings.

- *Be aware of linguistic bias in texts and course materials.* If you must use biased texts in your classroom, point out any problem expressions to your students and explain why such language is harmful.

Here are a number of concrete strategies you can use in the classroom to teach understanding and to help maintain your students' self-esteem and pride:

- Learn and teach the National Hate Crimes Act of 1990. This federal act requires law enforcement agencies all over the United States to report incidents of hate crimes motivated by prejudice—including those based on sexual orientation—to the Federal Bureau of Investigation and to investigate the crime.

- Inform students that they have the right to report incidents of name-calling, gay-bashing, and violence based on sexual orientation. Teachers, principals, and other adults have a responsibility to encourage students to report harassment to the police, or to report it themselves (Pollack and Schwartz, 1995).

⚘ Every school district in this country has a student conduct policy which includes the prohibition of harassment. There are, unfortunately, incidences of teachers singling out students who are gay or lesbian for verbal abuse, of individual and gang attacks, and of more subtle discrimination by teachers and students alike. As a teacher you should know and enforce the rules of behavior, and make them known to your students (Pollack and Schwartz, 1995). Both the National Education Association and the American Federation of Teachers have issued policy statements which call for an end to harassment and the establishment of support groups for gay and lesbian students.

⚘ Be aware that there are gay and lesbian students in your classroom, invisible or not. There are also always students who have a gay or lesbian parent, friend, or relative. Your acknowledgment of their reality is meaningful to them.

⚘ Set clear and firm rules in your classroom against slurs and discrimination. Consider posting the law against hate crimes. Discuss the need for such laws. State specifically your policy of inclusion, naming each group. A sample policy statement is provided in the appendix to this worktext.

⚘ Use inclusive language in writing and in conversation. Rather than asking a girl, "Do you have a boyfriend?" say "Is there anyone special you're seeing?"

⚘ In a classroom exercise, ask students collectively to list some examples of stereotypes about sex and gender that they hear regularly. These can come from friends, television, movies, etc. List these on one side of the board or a poster. On the other side, list examples which prove the stereotype false. For example: "Girls don't do math well." Proof that that is false: "Your math teacher is female."

⚘ Dispel stereotypes relating to gender and sexual orientation, such as the ones listed below:

• There are certain jobs which girls cannot do.
• Boys are more athletic than girls.
• Only gay people get AIDS.
• It's easy to tell someone's sexual orientation.
• Girls just like to talk on the phone and shop.
• Blondes are stupid.
• Girls who carry condoms are sluts.
• Boys who have sex are studs.
• Boys who cry are sissies.
• Girls who cry are sensitive.

- Boys who are not sexually active are homosexual.
- Girls who are sexually active are tramps.
- Girls who are athletic are lesbians.
- Girls who dress in men's clothing are fashionable.
- Boys who dress flamboyantly are gay.

❦ Teach that common stereotypical language tends to demean people. Many common terms and labels are demeaning in most contexts, and they encourage divisiveness and generalizations. Remove negative terms from your vocabulary and from your classroom.

❦ Provide support to students who are struggling with their sexual orientation. Many schools and school districts have developed support groups for these students.

CLASSROOM
SIMULATION

Finally, let's return to the scenario that opened this chapter. Read the situation below and record your reactions. Answering the questions will prepare you to handle religious diversity in the classroom. There is no one "right" answer.

Setting: Your classroom
Time: Mid-morning
Persons involved: Your entire class in general, Tom is particular.
Background: Your class has been preparing for a school play for weeks. Today the costume shipment has arrived, to the excitement of your students.
Circumstances: You are distributing costumes to individual students. The boys' and girls' costumes all include tights to cover their legs.
Simulation: After everyone has opened up their costumes, you hear Tom, one of the lead actors in the play, loudly announce that he will not participate. "There's no way I'm wearing these panty hose," he exclaims, holding up a pair of black tights. "I'm not dressing like some queer!" The class goes into an uproar.

1. What are your objectives?

_____

_____

_____

_____

2. What is the first thing you will say to Tom?

_____

_____

_____

3. What will you say to Tom's parents?

_____

_____

_____

4. What will you say to your class as a whole?

_____

_____

_____

5. How might you prevent such a reaction in the future?

_____

_____

_____

CONCLUSION    Because the classroom, like the home, is the source of children's concepts about sex and gender, it is important to teach students to be comfortable with themselves and to defend themselves both psychologically and verbally against the disapproval of their peers and adults. It is helpful to address issues of sex and gender directly, acknowledging and discussing the fact that many people have ideas about what it means to be a boy or a girl which are wrong.

Teachers should make it clear that everyone is entitled to an opinion, but no one is entitled to cause pain to others. It is also useful to provide role models by bringing into the school and the classroom examples of men, women, and older children who have overcome biases and transcended sex or gender prejudice and are enjoying their choices.

The varieties of human sexuality defy easy categorization, even though labels are pervasive in our society. Though a minority of people participate in strictly heterosexual and strictly homosexual activities, most others fall somewhere in the middle. Biases about gender, sexual orientation, and men's and women's "natural roles" have led to sexual discrimination. Until we remove sexist attitudes from ourselves and sexism from our classrooms and other institutions, human beings will continue to be limited (Hanmer, 1990).

REFERENCES

Bass, E. & Kaufman, K. (1996). *Free your mind: The book for gay, lesbian, and bisexual youth—and their allies.* New York: Harper Perennial.

Ekstrand, M. (1995). Stereotypes. In *Healthy Oakland teens project: 1995-1996 curriculum.* [On-line.] Available: http://www.epibiostat.ucsf.edu/capsweb/curricula/peer4.html

Gallagher, J. (1994). 10%: reality or myth? *The Advocate* 15 Nov., 23.

Hanmer, T. J. (1990). *Taking a stand against sexism and sex discrimination.* New York: Franklin Watts.

Myers, D. G. (1995). *Psychology.* New York: Hope.

Pollack, R. & Schwartz, C. (1995). *The journey out: A guide for and about lesbian, gay, and bisexual teens.* New York: Viking.

Reiss, B. F. (1980). Psychological tests in homosexuality. In J. Marmor, (Ed.), *Homosexual behavior* (pp. 296-311). New York: Basic Books.

Schuman, D. & Olufs, D. (1995). *Diversity on campus.* Boston: Allyn and Bacon.

Shargel, S. & Kane, I. (1974). *We can change it!* New York: Change for Children.

Notes

# Religious Diversity in the Classroom

**5**

OBJECTIVES

By the end of this chapter you should be able to answer these questions:

- What does religion mean?
- What are the major and minor belief systems of the world?
- What steps can you take to foster your students' understanding of people who follow different religions?
- How can you help each student to view his or her own personal religion in a universal context?

THE CLASSROOM IS A MICROCOSM

*The parents of Scott, a Native American student in your class, have scheduled a conference with you. Their son's "medicine bundle"—a sacred bag containing feathers, birds' beaks, oddly shaped stones, and tobacco leaves—has been stolen by his classmates, purportedly for the tobacco. The parents explain that every object in Scott's bag had a unique religious significance and called for a special song when its owner exposed it to the light. They say that this violation of Scott's sacred bag amounts to a desecration of his tribal religion. Typically a happy and outgoing student, Scott has been despondent since the incident.*

INTRODUCTION

Religion involves powerfully-charged feelings, passionate dedications, and deep loyalties. Religion is as old as humankind. In a very real sense, the history of humankind has been driven by religion. In the name of religion, wars have been fought, new territories have been discovered, and conflicts have been resolved. Though there are myriad expressions of spirituality across the globe, the underlying religious impulse is shared by all faiths.

### World Membership of Major Religions

| | |
|---|---|
| Christians | 1,900,174,000 |
| Moslems | 1,033,453,000 |
| Nonreligious | 924,078,000 |
| Hindus | 764,000,000 |
| Buddhists | 338,621,000 |
| Atheists | 239,111,000 |
| Taoists, Chinese folk beliefs | 190,000,000 |
| New Religionists | 128,975,000 |
| Tribal | 99,150,000 |
| Shamanists | 11,010,000 |
| Sikhs | 10,204,000 |
| Jews | 13,451,000 |
| Confucians | 6,334,000 |
| Baha'is | 5,835,000 |
| Jains | 3,987,000 |
| Shintoists | 3,387,800 |
| Other religionists | 20,419,000 |

Caution: Definitions of membership vary greatly from one religious body to another. For example, some count children who have been received into the faith, and others count only adults (Johnson, 1995).

61

Our culture is enriched by religious traditions. The passing of our years is marked by festivals, rituals, and holidays which honor figures and events from many faiths. Name two such holidays that are celebrated by different religious groups:

1. _____

2. _____

Such celebrations typically involve special costumes, foods, dances, and songs. Describe the special traditions associated with the holidays you named above:

1. _____

_____

2. _____

_____

The repetition of religious stories has kept alive some of the world's finest literature through the ages. Much of the most beautiful architecture and art in the world, from the pyramids in Egypt to the Sistine Chapel in Rome, have come from our attempt to express religious feelings. Name your favorite story, example of architecture, or piece of art which expresses religious feeling:

_____

_____

> **VOICES OF EXPERIENCE**
>
> *"Tolerance implies no lack of commitment to one's own beliefs. Rather, it condemns the oppression or persecution of others."*
> —John F. Kennedy, President of the U.S.

Religion clearly influences our lives in tangible ways—indeed, there's no escaping it. The moral and ethical underpinnings of our society are based on these ancient beliefs. Teachers have the important responsibility of educating about religious culture. What your students learn about religious art, stories, festivals, and rituals will fuel their respect and appreciation for different points of view. Understanding other belief systems will help each student to better understand his or her own beliefs and to improve interactions with all people.

Not all religions survive. The gods of Ancient Greece, for instance, are no longer worshipped. It takes people to keep a religion alive, and people incorporate religion into their daily lives in such profound ways that we are often unaware of them. People of many faiths welcome the coming of spring with a religious-based holiday, the harvest with a thanksgiving feast, and the new year with a celebration often related to religious beliefs. Even those who profess no faith usually participate in rituals which have their roots in religion. Can you think of a few?

_____

_____

Weddings, funerals, and baby-showers all have their roots in religious rituals.

PERSPECTIVE ONE

Religion has been defined as the attitude of individuals in a community toward the powers which they conceive as having ultimate control over their destinies and interests (Lewis, 1968). But don't let that definition confuse you. Religion is simply the part of culture associated with people's deepest convictions. Through religion we seek to explain awe-inspiring, mysterious concepts: What is God? Why does evil exist? Is there a soul? What happens when we die? How did humanity begin and when, if ever, will it end? People need general ideas that give meaning to their lives by explaining their place in the universe. Different religions attempt to give different answers to these human questions.

There is talk today that the world is becoming one and that people are uniting under a "New World Order." Innovations in technology are certainly tying people together. Can you think of a specific example?

_____

Over the worldwide computer Internet, for example, a Baptist student in Kansas can bump into a Buddhist student in Japan and strike up a conversation. Although we live in a "global village," not everyone agrees about how to live, how to govern, or how to worship. Yet if we intend to live together, we must understand each other's deepest convictions.

The majority of the world's population adheres to one of four religious categories: Hinduism, Buddhism, Judeo-Christianity, or Islam. In order to appreciate and understand another belief system, your students will not necessarily need to agree with it. Rather, they will need to seek to understand and respect the differing viewpoint and the person who holds it.

63

It is impossible in this context to fully discuss every religion practiced in the world, much less the particular denominations and offshoots within each religion. However, a brief overview of the world's major belief systems is practical and useful. The following summaries, therefore, are intended to introduce some key concepts at the foundation of each religion.

### Animism/Shamanism

Animism and Shamanism are religious systems typically found in the tribal societies of Africa, Australia, and North and South America. Animism is a belief that God is present everywhere, in a multiplicity of expressions that inhabit natural objects such as rocks and trees and rivers. All beings and things were created by God and can be used for either good or bad purposes. Gifted people called Shamen (priests, prophets, medicine men) believe they can go into a visionary state and communicate with the great power of the universe. Such a communion helps to sustain nature and the relationship between human beings and the universe.

### Buddhism

Buddhists are found in the greatest numbers in eastern Asia. Buddhism is a religion founded by Buddha, a prince who lived in India several hundred years before Jesus. This prince renounced his wealth and status and began teaching a philosophy of physical discipline, moderation, silent contemplation (meditation), and universal brotherhood as a means of liberation from the physical world. Buddhists believe that our desires trap us in the "Wheel of Life," a cycle of rebirths. The goal of the Buddhist is to attain Nirvana, a state of complete peace and bliss in which one is free from the inability to fulfill desire.

### Christianity

Christianity has its roots in Judaism. Christianity is a religion of love, compassion, and fellowship, based on the life and teachings of Jesus Christ. Christianity sees God as a trinity—the mystery of three in one. Christians believe that Jesus is the Messiah (or savior) sent by God. They believe that Jesus, by dying and being resurrected, made up for the sin of Adam and thus redeemed the world, allowing all who believe in Him to enter Heaven. Christians rely on the *Bible* as the inspired word of God.

### Confucianism

Confucianism is a system of ethics based upon the teachings of Confucius. This system has dominated Chinese culture for 2,000 years. Confucius emphasized moral perfection for the individual and social order for society. He believed world harmony could be attained if people possessed such virtues as loyalty, respect, integrity, piety, righteousness, wisdom, benevolence, and courage. While Confucianism is not strictly a religion, its followers are certainly religious. Confucianism has no priesthood, churches, or system of gods, but Confucius himself is revered and worshipped as the ideal man, and Confucians believe that the goodness in human nature comes from Heaven.

### Hinduism

Hinduism, a religion of India, is one of the world's oldest living religions. Its holy scriptures, the *Rig-Veda*, date all the way back to 4000 B.C. and make reference to the genesis of the universe. Hindus believe in a personal creator God who sustains the universe. They follow the principle of Karma, a law of cause and effect in which every action one does, whether good or bad, eventually comes back to him or her. Hindus also believe in reincarnation, a cycle of never-ending births and deaths in which ignorant people are reborn according to the deeds (or Karma) of their past lives. Enlightened people are not reborn. Hindus see the material world as being an illusion which can be changed by one's viewpoint. They also believe that all people are actually facets of Brahman, the eternal web of the universe.

### Islam

Islam is the dominant faith in the Arab nations and is growing in other parts of the world. Like Christianity, Islam has its roots in Judaism and worships the same indivisible God (called Allah in Arabic). Islam was founded by Mohammed, a prophet (messenger) of God who dictated the *Koran.* The fundamental belief of Islam is that "There is only one God, and Mohammed is his prophet." The word *Islam* means "submission to the will of God." Followers of Mohammed, called Moslems, are obliged to pray five times a day, to avoid pork and alcohol, to give to the poor, and to make a pilgrimage to Mecca (Mohammed's birthplace) at least once in their lives.

### Jainism

Jainism is a native religion of India, founded by a man named Mahavira. This religion grew out of Hinduism and teaches a doctrine of non-injury, or *ahimsa.* Jains believe in the law of Karma (cause and effect) and reincarnation. Jains do not eat meat, and they seek to avoid harming anything believed to have a soul. Jains attempt to achieve *moksha,* or salvation, through self-discipline, knowledge, faith, and right conduct.

### Judaism

Judaism, the religion of the Hebrews, centers around a personal God, Yahweh. A succession of great prophets (spiritual messengers), such as Abraham, Moses, Elijah, and Isaiah, spoke in God's name and taught Jews how to know and serve Yahweh. In Judaism, a permanent covenant with God and his chosen people allows heaven to come to earth. Jewish law, legend, and history is embodied in the *Talmud* and the *Torah*. Jewish worship takes place in a synagogue and is led by a rabbi (a scholar of Jewish thought).

### Shinto

Shinto is the national religion of Japan. The word *Shinto* means "The Way of the Gods." Many Gods are honored, representing natural forces, ancestors, former emperors, and national heroes. Over 100,000 shrines have been built to the Gods. However, these shrines are not meant for the assembling of worshippers but rather as dwellings for the Gods. Many of the shrines are very small and are focal points for festivals and patriotic holidays. Shinto promotes national loyalty.

### Sikhism

Sikhism is a faith that arose in India as a result of the coming of Islam. It features elements of Islam and Hinduism, but maintains a separate identity. The founder of the movement was named Nanak. He taught that the way of salvation was through *bhakti* (devotion). Sikhs worship Hari, the one God. Sikhs believe in reincarnation and hope to break out of an endless cycle of rebirths to merge with the soul of God. The sacred book of the Sikhs, the *Granth*, contains Nanak's poems and songs of devotion.

### Taoism and Chinese Folk Religion

Taoism is a philosophical religion native to China. It was founded by a great philosopher named Lao Tse. Taoists attempt to live according to the Tao (pronounced *DOW*), or "Way," which they believe governs the

> ### Spotlight
> #### on the Classroom
>
> *"I always thought talk about religious persecution was just paranoia until last year, when the son of a friend of mine was chased by a gang of his sixth grade classmates and beaten up. The boy is Jewish and some boys in his class started playing a game called "Nazis." They had all been friends before, but now they targeted him to harass for fun.*
>
> *"The teacher sat them all down and told them about what Nazism is about and explained what Judaism is. They discussed the importance of religious freedom and so on, and the games stopped, at least at school.*
>
> *"I know that my little friend will never take his safety for granted again, though, and neither will I. There is so much fear of anything different from the majority, and it is so near the surface. The scariest thing is that wherever you go in the world, somebody is different."*
> —Anna M., parent

universe. Lao Tse called for people to be peaceful, inactive, and quiet. He believed that bringing these qualities into daily life would put one effortlessly in touch with the universe. The *Tao Te Ching*, or Book of the Way, spells out the doctrine of Lao Tse. Chinese folk religions combine Taoism, Buddhism, Confucianism, ancestor worship, and local deities.

### New Religions

New Religions have grown up in Asia, mostly since 1945. Some of these popular new beliefs were inspired by Buddhism and Shintoism. They were founded by visionaries who preached a fresh new social ethic. Most stress gratitude for God's creation, social rather than individual good, and hard manual labor. The Nichiren Shosu religion, founded in Japan earlier this century, has spread to other countries in both the East and the West.

PERSPECTIVE
TWO

Within the major religious systems are numerous denominations, all with their own special beliefs and practices. For example, Christianity is divided into four main denominations: Catholic, Protestant, Orthodox, and Anglican. Each of those is divided into smaller affiliations—Methodist, Baptist, Lutheran, Pentecostal, Presbyterian, Seventh-Day Adventist, Jehovah's Witness, Greek Orthodox, Shaker, and so on.

In addition to the major religions, there are dozens of minor religions, branches, and offshoots, including:

**Celtic religions**. These include the ancient nature cults of Great Britain, such as Druidism.

**Caribbean religions**. These religions of the Caribbean islands include Voodoo and Santeria. Though frequently misunderstood and stereotyped, Caribbean religions have a unique and rich cultural heritage.

**Eckanar**. Eckanar focuses on the personal experience of the sound and light of God.

**Esoteric Brotherhoods**. These exclusive, philosophical societies include the Rosicrucians and the Freemasons. They have a long history, dating back to ancient times.

**Krishna Consciousness**. Originating in India, this movement was made popular in the West during the 1960s by A. C. Bhaktivedanta Swami Prabhupada. It focuses on love, service, and devotion to Krishna, the personal aspect of God. Followers of Krishna avoid eating meat, engaging in illicit sex, the use of intoxicants, and gambling. They frequently chant the name of God (Prabhupada, 1969).

**Magick systems**. The ancient practice of Witchcraft is a magick system. Though often confused with Satanism, many magick systems practice "white magic" and stress personal empowerment through the energy of nature.

**Natural Law systems**. These are not religions in terms of doctrines or dogmas. Practitioners of these systems view individual life from a universal perspective. Based upon modern and ancient science and reports of higher states of consciousness, they recognize the intelligence and creativity underlying the order in the universe. Such a recognition offers one the choice regarding a personal relationship with the divine. Practitioners observe the natural rhythms and cycles of the universe, including the cycle of creation-maintenance-evolution-dissolution. The Transcendental Meditation movement, developed by Maharishi Mahesh Yogi, is a natural law system which can be followed from within any religious tradition (Yogi, 1972).

**North, Central, and South American Indigenous Religions**. These are ancient regional belief systems, many of which are tribal in origin. Followers of these religions are usually descended from a particular area's native population.

**Satanism**. Satanism is the worship of the Devil.

**Scientology**. This movement, founded by L. Ron Hubbard, teaches a modern science of mental health and social betterment.

**Spiritualist systems**. These systems include New Age beliefs (such as channeling).

**Sufism**. This is a system of Islamic mysticism which teaches that repentance, abstinence, poverty, patience, and trust lead to union with God. Love is the key to Sufi ethics. Some Sufis, called dervishes, engage in a devotional exercise which involves a whirling dance.

**Unification Church**. The Unification Church was established in Korea by the Rev. Sun Myung Moon in 1954 to bring about spiritual and social reform.

**Zoroastrianism**. This is a religion founded in Iran, based upon the philosophy of a man named Zoroaster. Zoroastrians worship the god Ahura Mazda, creator of goodness and light, and view life as a constant battle between good and evil. Good thoughts and deeds are the keys to salvation.

There are, of course, people who do not adhere to any faith at all. Some people call themselves skeptics or Agnostics. Agnosticism is a denial of knowledge about whether or not there is a God. People who are agnostic are open to the possibility that God exists but believe that there can be no proof either way. Other people, called Atheists, go so far as to reject all religions outright. Atheism is the denial that there is any God, no matter how God is defined.

On the opposite end of the spectrum, there are people who follow the wisdom of more than one faith. The Unitarian and Universalist movements, for example, tolerate various religious beliefs and study both Eastern and Western spiritual writings in a quest for universal brotherhood. Similarly, the Baha'i faith (which originated in Iran) emphasizes the spiritual unity of all humankind. A movement called Ecumenism promotes worldwide unity among churches and religions through greater cooperation and improved understanding. Another specialized church is the Metropolitan Community Church, which is an international Christian-based church for persons who are lesbian, gay, or bisexual, and their friends and family.

PERSPECTIVE
THREE
While religion is often a source of celebration, it sometimes fuels strife as well. In what way is religious prejudice different from racial prejudice?

_____

_____

Unlike racial prejudice, religious prejudice is directed against groups that people *choose* to join as a matter of faith (Kronenwetter, 1993). You will occasionally encounter religious prejudice in the classroom. At those times you may desire to teach that the following stereotypes about people of different faiths are *not* true:

- They are ignorant or unenlightened
- They are misguided
- They are sinful, ungodly, or devil-worshippers
- They are strange
- They are fanatics
- They want to convert you to their religion
- Their religious heritage is primitive
- They hate people who don't adhere to their faith

Religious prejudice stems from the belief that one's particular faith is favored by God. Ironically, virtually all of the world's religions teach against prejudice in favor of tolerance, unity, and love.

In addition to the major and minor world religions defined in this chapter, it is useful to be familiar with these other related terms:

**Belief.** This refers to faith and trust in the truth or existence of something abstract or intangible.

**Conviction.** This is an earnest and profound belief in something, such as religious doctrines.

**Creed.** A creed is an accepted system of religious belief. The word is derived from the Latin *credo*, meaning "I believe."

**Doctrine.** This is a particular principle taught by a religion.

**Dogma.** This refers to a set of firmly established doctrines authoritatively put forth by a particular church.

**Faith.** This refers to a belief in God or the teachings of a particular religion. This word is also used to mean a system of religious belief, as in "the Jewish faith."

**Persecution.** This refers to the act of oppressing, injuring, subjugating, and/or exterminating someone for adhering to a particular religious faith.

**Religion.** This is a belief system that seeks to explain one's place in the universe.

Following are some helpful guidelines that you can share with your students to foster their understanding of religious diversity. These guidelines are appropriate for students of any faith and will empower both them and you to have better interactions with everyone:

● *Resist trying to force others with another faith into the categories of your own belief system.* Take them on their own terms, giving their experiences and beliefs respect.

● *If another religion seems foreign or confusing, remember that it is simply another human attempt to make sense of life's mysteries.* Keep in mind that *your* belief system may seem just as foreign to someone who doesn't follow it.

● *Before you form an opinion about a believer of another faith, remember the key quality you have in common.* Both of you carry on the tradition of a long line of believers stretching back through time.

✦ *Do not be embarrassed by your ignorance of a person's faith and customs.* Ask questions in an open, friendly, interested manner and you are likely to find that the person will be eager to discuss and share his or her religious culture.

✦ *Approach another religion in the light of what it contributes to the life of its followers.* Ask followers of this religion how their faith has changed their lives, or empowered them, or comforted them. Ask how religious holidays involve the participation of their families.

CLASSROOM
STRATEGIES
Though the subject of religion can seem impossibly vast, here are a number of concrete strategies you can use in the classroom to teach understanding and to help maintain your students' self-esteem and pride:

✦ Throughout the school year, highlight important holidays of as many religions as possible. Discuss the customs, special clothing, food, symbols, and activities associated with each.

✦ Conduct frank discussions about religious persecution. Consider showing one of several compelling films about Anne Frank, the young Jewish girl who wrote her famous diary while in hiding from the Nazis.

✦ Discuss common religious stereotypes and examine why each is untrue. These stereotypes are often found in the mass media. Have groups investigate what is being reported and develop their own "factual" version of the story.

✦ Invite guest speakers devout in particular faiths who have found careers that allow for observance of and participation in their religion. Encourage the speakers to explain any special clothing or other symbols that they wear in pride and honor of their faith.

✦ Have students report on famous leaders who are or were devout in a particular faith, such as Martin Luther King, Jr., Mother Theresa, Mahatma Gandhi, Malcom X, Billy Graham, or the Dalai Lama.

✦ When discussing diverse belief systems, build upon what your students already know. Always start with familiar terminology, and highlight similarities before pointing out differences.

✦ An excellent way to combat religious prejudice is to suggest visiting the church of another faith. Your students will notice that every religion has a system of rituals or ceremonies, no matter how elaborate or simple. Candles may be lit, prayers said, or food offered. Even a bowed head, folded hands, and the repetition of sacred words are ceremonial. Have your students describe a ceremony they witness. Discuss in what ways is it similar to or different from a ceremony with which they are more familiar.

♦ Be sensitive to making your school's attendance policy flexible for students involved in religious celebrations and/or duties (Cushner, McClelland, & Safford, 1996).

♦ Regarding your school's dress code, make allowances for religiously-based customs and regulations. For example, some schools prohibit the wearing of hats, but an Orthodox Jewish boy may wear a yarmulke as a token of his respect for God, or an Amish girl may wear a dimity bonnet and long dress as a gesture of modesty (Cushner, McClelland, & Safford, 1996).

♦ Be aware not to make assumptions about your students' beliefs. STOP and consider whether your statements are sensitive to other belief systems than your own.

CLASSROOM SIMULATION

Finally, let's return to the scenario that opened this chapter. Read the situation below and record your reactions. Answering the questions will prepare you to handle religious diversity in the classroom. There is no one "right" answer.

| | |
|---:|:---|
| Setting: | Your classroom |
| Time: | The end of the day |
| Persons involved: | The parents of Scott, a Native American student |
| Background: | Scott's medicine bag, a holy symbol of his tribal religion, was stolen yesterday. Scott, a normally outgoing student, was despondent all day today. |
| Circumstances: | You are meeting Scott's parents in a conference. |
| Simulation: | Scott's father says: "This act of theft was a devastating blow to our son and to us. The medicine bundle has sacred meaning. This theft is nothing less than a desecration of our religion. You say that our son is despondent now. How *should* he act in a classroom that exhibits such utter disrespect for religion?" |

1. What are your objectives?

_____

_____

_____

72

2. What is the first thing you will say to Scott's father?

_____

_____

_____

3. What will you say to Scott the next day?

_____

_____

_____

4. What will you say to your class the next day?

_____

_____

_____

5. Outside of disciplinary procedures, how might you prevent such an occurrence from happening again?

_____

_____

_____

_____

Religion is a universal experience of awe and wonder in the presence of the mysterious. In different lands and different times, throughout human history, religion has helped people to understand their lives in a larger, cosmic context. Religion concerns the deepest and most sensitive area of a person's experience. The only way for your students to be sympathetic and objective toward others of another faith is for them to be knowledgeable about different belief systems.

Perhaps people will never agree about the fine points of religious doctrine, but such agreement is not necessary. One does not have to convert to another religion in order to honor the piety of its followers. Your challenge as a teacher is to practice what you preach. Do you believe that your actions will one day be judged by God, or that your deeds in this life will come back to you the next time around, or that you are answerable only to yourself?

_____

_____

_____

No matter how we express it, virtually everyone agrees that people are all accountable for their actions. Whether all humankind are facets of God, or part of the web of the universe, or descendants of Adam, everyone is entitled to respect. Regardless of our religion or lack thereof, we are all travelers on the journey of life. Teach your students that if they are convinced that theirs is the best path, they should strive to be respectable representatives and give others the opportunity to be drawn to their example.

REFERENCES Cushner, K, McClelland, A., & Safford, P. (1996). *Human diversity in education: An integrative approach.* New York: McGraw-Hill.

Johnson, O. (1995). *1996 information please almanac.* Boston: Houghton Mifflin Company.

Kronenwetter, M. (1993). *Prejudice in America: Causes and cures.* New York: Franklin Watts.

Lewis, J. (1968). *Religions of the world made simple.* Garden City, NY: Doubleday.

Prabhupada, A. C. B. S. (1969). *Sri Isopanisad.* Los Angeles: Bhaktivendanta Book Trust.

Yogi, M. M. (1972). *The science of creative intelligence: Teacher training course.* Fairfield, IA: Maharishi International University.

# Socioeconomics in the Classroom

OBJECTIVES    By the end of this chapter, you should be able to answer these questions:

- ◖ In what ways does socioeconomic status affect a student's self-concept?
- ◖ What is the relationship between economic disadvantage and academic underachievement?
- ◖ What are the ways in which society determines socioeconomic status?
- ◖ What are the ways that teachers can help students to overcome socioeconomic stereotypes?
- ◖ How can socioeconomic differences in the classroom be minimized?

THE CLASSROOM IS A MICROCOSM

*You have just announced the exciting news that there will be a class trip to a nearby theme park next month. While passing out permission slips and information letters for the class to take home to parents, one of your best-mannered students, Carl, says loudly, "This trip sucks—I'm not going," and begins making rude noises. You immediately realize that Carl knows his family can't afford the $35 ticket, though it is a school discount.*

INTRODUCTION    The importance of the term *socioeconomic diversity* is clear from its name. We add the prefix "socio" because economics affects our status, or place in society, and therefore colors every aspect of our lives. The level of our wealth or poverty can lessen or increase our chances of overcoming other differences. Wealth gives us access to services, advantages, and opportunities which are unavailable to those who are poor, and it can break down social barriers because people often put money before other biases.

The term *socioeconomic status* describes the place in a society where a person's income, level of education, or occupation places him or her. The United States Bureau of the Census is responsible for measuring economic conditions using these criteria. In this chapter we will look at data on the socioeconomic status of children and consider how wealth and poverty are related to some education issues which affect us all. We will look at societal

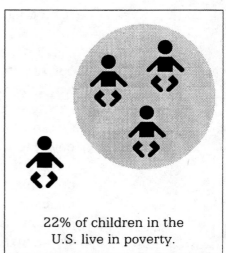

22% of children in the U.S. live in poverty.

attitudes about wealth and poverty and consider how cultural norms may change our definitions of those terms. We will see that labeling and stereotyping in regard to socioeconomic status are as harmful as any other labeling and stereotyping, and as mistaken a notion. Finally, we will look at how we can overcome our biases and better address the needs of our students.

PERSPECTIVE ONE

Our socioeconomic status determines to a large degree the ways in which we are perceived by others and the way we view ourselves. What are some examples of the ways in which socioeconomic status affects a student's self-concept?

_____

_____

_____

Students may compare themselves unfavorably with classmates who have more economic advantages. They may feel that their status reflects upon them personally, and that they are less likely to succeed.

What are some ways in which socioeconomic status affects how students are perceived by their classmates?

_____

_____

_____

Students might look to more affluent classmates for leadership, confusing social status with competence. There might also be scapegoating or exclusion based on socioeconomic status.

One can acquire prestige and popularity in a number of ways in our society. According to sociologist Tim North (1994), one important way to acquire prestige is by occupation. Employment as a laborer, for example, probably offers less prestige than employment as a surgeon. A stereotype we have about laborers is that they are less educated and have less wealth than, say, a physician. If we think before we make this assumption, however, we realize that a laborer may also *be* a surgeon, or a musician, or a writer. The surgeon may have more or less education, more or fewer skills, and be rich or poor. The great humanitarian Mother Teresa is a small, frail, elderly, unemployed woman who dresses very simply and lives in an impoverished section of the city, among the ill.  By stereotypical standards, what should her status be?

_____

Think for a moment about your own prejudices about occupations.  Are you aware of how your fellow students' parents earn their living?

_____

Were you aware of what your classmates' parents did for a living when you were a child?

_____

_____

How do you think this affected your perception of your friends?

_____

_____

_____

Did you think some of them were more likely to go to college because their parents had gone to college?

_____

Consider the following question carefully before you answer it.  To what extent do you believe that the value of work is related to its compensation in our society?

_____

_____

Why do you think teaching is one of the lower paid professions?

_____

_____

_____

It might be helpful to discuss occupations with your students, emphasizing their value to society, the skills which they involve, and the fact that most of us have many occupations in our lives.

Perspective
Two

Another way that we award status is by appearance, or dress, and this can have tremendous impact in the classroom. We may make assumptions about a student's socioeconomic status based on whether he or she is wearing combat boots, cowboy boots, sneakers, or high heels. We may judge by the brand names on the child's clothing, or by his or her hairstyle. We all use these superficial clues to assess status, and they can be useful tools in learning about the child. They can be deceiving, however. A popular style among students a few years ago was wearing hospital greens. As we have seen in our examination of other kinds of stereotyping, it is always a mistake to judge by appearances. For instance, your grandmother might look at rock singer Axl Rose, of Guns 'N' Roses, and think that he is a poor, unemployed street person.

How do you think school uniforms would affect stereotyping by dress?

_____

_____

_____

Students might find other ways to signal their socioeconomic status. They might wear expensive jewelry, for example.

In the same way that prejudicial judgments may be made based on clothing or occupation, status is often assigned according to where people live. One's address may be seen is an indicator of wealth or poverty. As evidenced by a popular television show of the early 1990s, *Beverly Hills 90210*, a zip code alone can be a kind of code for a way of life or for a certain socioeconomic status which represents a lifestyle. Within that sequence of numbers is contained assumptions about how a group of people is likely to think, behave, dress, and interact. That zip code evokes in the viewer an assumption that the residents live in large houses, drive expensive cars, and have particular occupations. Similarly, an earlier television series, *Dallas*, focused on stereotypes about wealthy Texans, while *All in the Family* and *Roseanne* centered around lower class working families.

We can all enjoy these representations of socioeconomic stereotypes, and can recognize familiar patterns, but as with all other instances in which we judge individuals based on stereotypes, we risk making hurtful and harmful mistakes, and we stand a good chance of impeding both the growth of our own understanding and the progress of society toward gaining the potential benefits of inclusion. Many university students might suffer from false assumptions based on zip code since they often live in lower rent areas, sometimes in crowded conditions and without the amenities they have at their parents' homes. Younger students may bear the stigma of their parents' address. What are some ways in which we, as teachers, can help our students to overcome stereotypical thinking?

_____

_____

_____

It can be useful to point out how we have arrived at our ideas about dress and occupation. Students might become more aware of the judgments they are unconsciously making by looking at magazine photos of individuals, trying to guess their jobs or income, and then stating their reasons for that guess. It usually quickly becomes clear to the student that he or she is being influenced by superficial signals. The goal is to look beyond the superficial exterior and see the individual.

PERSPECTIVE THREE

How susceptible are you to these same superficial signals? We can see the danger in making assumptions by looking at some statistics. According to the Bureau of the Census (1995), in 1990 more than 52 million Americans lived in areas where at least 20 percent of residents were poor. These areas are designated "poverty areas." However, most residents of poverty areas were not poor. Though these areas have high concentrations of poor people, statistics show that 69 percent were actually above the poverty line. More than half the people living in poverty areas were white.

> **VOICES OF EXPERIENCE**
>
> *"I lost my job six months ago. My kids do not have any shoes, and I cannot afford to feed them every day. They don't complain, though. They're tough. We live in an abandoned building. I found all of our furniture on the streets. We have a table, a chair, a sofa, and a bed. I look for aluminum cans to sell for money. I worry about my kids when I am gone all day. I feel very sad all the time. I don't know where we will be tomorrow."*
> —Beth H., parent

In 1993, there were 39.3 million Americans below the official government poverty level. This number represents 15.1 percent of the nation's population. The poverty rate for children under 18 was 22.7 percent, and persons 18 through 64 years of age comprised 12.4 percent of the poor (Johnson, 1995). In a country as wealthy as the United States, would you expect less poverty than in other industrialized parts of the world?

_____

_____

According to economist Peter Montague (1994), the United States has a higher incidence of poverty than other industrialized countries such as Norway, West Germany, and Japan, with exceptionally high infant and child poverty.

There is a disparity by race in terms of socioeconomic status. Most recent Census statistics show that non-Hispanic Caucasians had a poverty rate of over 12 percent, while African Americans had a rate of over 33 percent. The largest representation of people of other races was Asians and Pacific Islanders in 1993, and their poverty rate was over 15 percent (Johnson, 1995). What would you guess the percentage of Caucasians to be?

_____

It is important to note that though the poverty rate for Caucasians was lower than for those of other races and ethnicity, they still made up the majority of families suffering poverty in the latest census.

> **Spotlight on the Classroom**
>
> *"Social status in my classroom takes some surprising twists. For instance, two students — one a reputed drug dealer, and the other a gang leader—have a great deal of money but occupy positions of low status. My students who achieved the three highest status positions are the cheerleading captain, the football star, and the high academic achiever. Their prestige has nothing to do with money."*
> —Rita P., teacher

Can you think of some categories of people whom you would assume to be economically disadvantaged?

_____

_____

According to the last Census, families with a female head of household still make up a majority of people living in poverty. Families maintained by a woman alone have a poverty rate of over 35 percent as compared to married couple households with a rate of nearly 7 percent. Children born in another country are over one and a half times as likely to be poor as native-born citizens. Recent immigrants are over twice as likely to be in poverty (Johnson, 1995).

Certain societal problems are directly attributable to poverty. Poverty breeds crime, disease, and illiteracy. What government programs are you aware of which address problems of poverty?

_____

_____

Do you know of programs which address the needs of economically disadvantaged children?

_____

_____

Governmental attempts to address the problems of poverty in our society include such programs as Head Start (a preschool program), the Food Stamp Program, the National School Lunch Program, the Low-Income Home Energy Assistance Program, Aid to Families with Dependent Children, and Supplemental Security Income (Bureau of the Census, 1995).

PERSPECTIVE
FOUR

Healthy, safe, secure children generally perform well in today's schools. However, according to Eugene Garcia (1994), economically disadvantaged students are three times more likely to drop out than those from more economically advantaged homes. Students living in economically disadvantaged or unsafe environments are at risk for academic underachievement both now and in the future (Garcia, 1994). Name some reasons that economically disadvantaged children may underachieve academically:

_____

_____

When children live in stressful, insecure environments they often have difficulty focusing and learning. Malnutrition, lack of sufficient sleep, and poor physical health may also play a role in academic underachievement.

The culture of school itself may be problematic for children from homes which are economically disadvantaged. They may be less competent and less confident linguistically due either to language differences or to limited exposure to reading or language skills. The very form or wording of questions may present a cultural challenge for these children (Cushner, McClelland, & Safford, 1996).

Quality of life can be measured in various ways, and teachers can help their students to realize this. The standard of well-being is different in a small village in Africa or Asia than it is in Los Angeles. What do you personally consider economic well-being?

_____

_____

_____

In thinking about our own socioeconomic status, we may consider the things we own, whether we can afford adequate housing, the safety of our neighborhoods, our ability to enjoy health and good nutrition, and our ability to earn a good income (Bureau of the Census, 1995). Clearly we are poor unless we have educational opportunities, health resources, and access to justice.

The impact of socioeconomic diversity in the classroom can be minimized by emphasizing human, rather than material values. It is important to point out to students that the possession of money, though empowering in many ways, is not an indicator of an individual's personality, taste, lifestyle, or value as a human being. What are some examples of persons who disproved our stereotypes?

_____

_____

_____

Billionaire Howard Hughes became a recluse at a young age and, by many accounts, lived much like a homeless person. Sam Walton, the super-wealthy founder of the WalMart stores, is said to have taken his lunch to work every day in a paper bag and in other ways continued to live as he had when he was poor.

Try to help your students think of wealth as a quality of life rather than the accumulation of money. Then they will see that it is possible to feel very wealthy without accumulating money. Demonstrate that there is value in simple pleasures, in knowledge, and in service to others. Many of the richest and most powerful people who have ever lived have discovered this fact and valued life more than wealth.

It is important to understand the following concepts relating to socioeconomic diversity:

**Lower class.** This refers to a segment of society which lives in poverty, sometimes called "the working poor."

**Lower middle class.** This refers to the largest segment of society, comprised mostly of white-collar workers employed in a variety of middle-income occupations.

**Social class.** This is an abstract concept which refers to a hierarchical layering of people into categories based upon their income, level of education, family name or bloodline, and influence.

**Social status.** This is determined by the prestige, esteem, and honor one is accorded within his or her own social milieu (Cushner, McClelland, & Safford, 1996).

**Underclass.** This refers to a segment of society which seems unable to take advantage of any mobility options and thus lies on the outskirts of the class system (Cushner, McClelland, & Safford, 1996).

**Upper class.** This refers to a small segment of society—the social elite— and is a position often inherited from one's family.

**Upper middle class.** This refers to a segment of society comprised mostly of highly educated professionals.

**Working class.** This refers to a segment of society comprised of blue-collar workers with low-paying industrial or service jobs.

EMPOWERMENT
TIPS

Here are some tips that you can share with your students to foster their understanding of socioeconomic diversity. Be a role model!

- *Be charitable.* Donate your excess to organizations which enhance life for those who have less.

- *Be active in your community.* Give some of your time and energy to help guarantee equal access to justice and education for those who live in poverty.

85

* *Be instrumental in stopping poverty at its roots.* Encourage children to learn to read, to be curious about life, and to participate in their own lives.

* *Be optimistic.* Remember that poverty is reversible. Help one individual at a time. Generosity is not dictated by the size of your bank account. You can give your support, your knowledge, your sense of humor, and your love.

* *Become more aware of your own wealth.* Appreciate the material advantages that you enjoy while increasing your understanding of what wealth really means. Poets, philosophers, spiritual and social leaders all teach us that money is not the measure of true wealth.

* *Be careful not to stereotype people based on superficial aspects such as clothing, zip code, or occupation.* Approach every individual respectfully.

Following are a number of helpful strategies you can use in a socioeconomically diverse classroom.

* Have each student bring five pennies to class. Play a game in which each student must give away as many pennies as possible to his or her classmates. As the game progresses, students will see that they cannot give away the pennies fast enough because more pennies keep coming back to them. You may want to point out that our economy is described in terms of "fluidity"—the constant flow of money among individuals. Explain that being affluent doesn't just mean being rich in dollars. It means being rich in generosity as well.

* Invite guest speakers who spread the wealth of human resources. Such organizations as Habitat for Humanity and Red Cross offer opportunities to show how students can help to fight poverty and at the same time show that very valuable gifts can come from one's own effort rather than a checkbook.

* Be aware of the cultural context of your classroom, your language, and written and spoken questions to students. Ask questions more than one way so that children are not penalized for differences in language or style and assessed inaccurately.

* Be sensitive in making class plans. All students may not be able to afford even minor expenses. Arrange fund-raising activities and pool resources to avoid embarrassing or excluding anyone. Make it "all or none."

- Be aware that some students may not have the resources for vision or hearing screening, or may be unable to buy glasses. Poor nutrition or an unstable home environment may mean too little rest or study time. Keep these factors in mind when you evaluate a student's performance.

- Demonstrate that wealth is not only money. Showcase student talent in art, music, storytelling, math, or any other area. Talk about contributions students make to each other or to the community by helping out or by offering a smile.

- Use current events as well as literature to draw attention to human values over material values. Encourage discussion about what our society seems to value most.

- Lead a discussion about what your students would do if they had "all the money in the world." What would they spend it on? Would they travel? Give to a particular charity? Support a certain cause? Fund a scholarship in a field of study? Shower gifts on friends and family? Your students can learn a lot about their real priorities by coming up with an honest answer. Andrew Carnegie used his wealth to establish libraries. Rockefeller endowed the arts. Discussing how one would spend all the money in the world helps you to clarify the idea of money itself.

- Talk about these common misconceptions about people who live in poverty. Point out that is not true that they:
  - Are usually homeless
  - Are prone to substance abuse
  - Have below-average intelligence
  - Are all unemployed
  - Are lazy
  - Are uneducated
  - Choose to live in poverty
  - Have no hope of escaping poverty
  - Were born into poverty
  - Have equal opportunity
  - Are not law-abiding
  - Are ineffective parents

- Talk about these common misconceptions about people who are wealthy. Point out that it is not true that they:
  - Are all hard workers
  - Are all shallow
  - Were born into wealth
  - Are all employed

- Are all greedy
- Are never generous
- Are always law-abiding
- Are never victims of crimes
- Have little social consciousness
- Have great social consciousness
- Are effective parents
- Are well-educated

CLASSROOM
SIMULATION

Finally, let's return to the scenario that opened this chapter. Read the situation below and record your reactions. Answering the questions will prepare you to handle socioeconomic diversity in the classroom. There is no one "right" answer.

Setting: Your classroom

Time: 9:30 a.m.

Persons involved: Carl, one of your best-mannered students, and the rest of his classmates

Background: You are aware that Carl's family has economic disadvantages.

Circumstances: You have just announced an upcoming class trip to a nearby theme park and are passing out permission slips for parents to sign.

Simulation: Carl says loudly, "This trip sucks—I'm not going." Then he begins making rude noises.

1. What are your objectives?

_____

_____

_____

2. What do you say to Carl?

_____

_____

_____

_____

3. What do you say to the class as a whole?

_____

_____

_____

4. What will you say to Carl's parents?

_____

_____

_____

5. How could you have avoided this situation?

_____

_____

_____

CONCLUSION

Be careful not to stereotype those who are economically advantaged any more than you do those who live in poverty. People who are considered wealthy often attend the best schools, have the finest medical care, and achieve professionally at the highest level due to status and connections. It happens, however, that children from the wealthiest group of citizens, like those from the poorest, are often mistrusted by the vast middle class of Americans. There is prejudice and resentment against both groups. Although wealth may bring with it the opportunity for a luxurious lifestyle, as it is often depicted on such television shows as *Lifestyles of the Rich and Famous*, it also brings problems, stereotypes, and stigmas. We must recognize that, no matter what their socioeconomic status, human beings all have the same physical, emotional, and intellectual needs. We should therefore address the needs of our students accordingly.

REFERENCES

Bureau of the Census. (1995). Income and poverty. *Census home page.* [On-line]. Available: http://www.census.gov/ftp/pub/hhes/www/incpov.html

Cushner, K., McClelland, A., & Safford, P. (1996). *Human diversity in education: An integrative approach.* New York: McGraw-Hill.

Garcia, E. (1994). *Understanding and meeting the challenge of student cultural diversity.* Boston: Houghton Mifflin Co.

Johnson, O. (Ed.). (1995). *1996 information please almanac.* Boston: Houghton Mifflin Company.

Montague, P. (1994). Economic trends. *Rachel's environment and health weekly.* [On-line]. Available: ftp.std.com/periodicals/rachel

North, T. (1994). Acquiring prestige and popularity. *The Internet and Usenet global computer networks: An investigation of their culture and its effects on new users.* [On-line]. Available: http://foo.curtain.edu.au/Thesis/Chap4b.html

# Physical Differences in the Classroom

**OBJECTIVES**  By the end of this chapter you should be able to answer these questions:

- What is the definition in schools of a physical disability?
- What does it mean to describe someone as having a physical difference?
- What are the various types of physical disabilities?
- What are some causes of physical disabilities and differences?
- What are good strategies for assisting people with physical disabilities in the classroom?

**THE CLASSROOM IS A MICROCOSM**  *You have been out sick for a day and return to the classroom to find your students full of questions about your substitute. To your surprise, two students have brought notes from their parents complaining about this teacher. Susan, a leader and opinion-maker in your class, greets you with "We're so glad you're back. Mr. Sanchez was weird. We didn't know what to say him. My mother says cripples shouldn't be allowed to teach." Fifteen hands are suddenly raised, all waving for your attention.*

**INTRODUCTION**  Ideas about which physical attributes are desirable vary from culture to culture and from time to time. Our concepts of beauty are very complex and complicated. We are influenced by art and advertising, among other things, in our attitudes toward physical differences.

*I am different.*

*This calls for a celebration!*

We know that all of us are different from each other and that people come in many sizes and shapes. Every day, babies are born who have physical disabilities. Many others of us suffer disabling accidents and illnesses. Still, society often poses challenges for people with physical differences because we tend to see the difference first and the person second. We live in a world which focuses on sameness.

When physical differences are shown on television, in movies, or in advertisements, they are often the subject of humor, such as the "*fat lady*," the "*short* man," or the "*ugly* child." Can you think of some particular celebrities whose physical differences are the subject of humor? List a few examples below:

_____

_____

Comedian John Candy's weight, singer Barbara Streisand's nose, and actor Danny DeVito's stature are all well known topics of humor, along with countless others. Even actress Elizabeth Taylor, universally thought to be one of the most beautiful women alive, has been derided and ridiculed when she gained weight.

PERSPECTIVE
ONE

The practice of reading a person's character from his or her facial and bodily form is not new. It dates back to the ancient Greeks and is still found in some parts of the world. We often judge a person's character by facial qualities, and our language expresses this. We say: "He has an open face," "She gave a frank look," "He had a sinister appearance," "She gave a furtive glance." The age-old art of interpreting physiognomy took all sorts of physical characteristics into account: one's stature, build, posture, forehead, nose, ears, chin, eyebrows, eyes, cheeks, mouth, and hair. Bumps on the head were also interpreted (in a pseudo-science called "Phrenology,") as were lines on the palm of the hand ("Palmistry"). Today, we never make judgments on such superficial bases. Or do we?

People do sometimes fall into general "body types," and certain characteristics *are* associated with physical features. The study of this phenomenon is called morphology. For thousands of years and up to the present day, the traditional medical practitioners of China and India have relied upon morphology to classify and treat their patients. Do you fall into one of these three morphological categories? Underline all the

| Type 1 | Type 2 | Type 3 |
|---|---|---|
| Moderate frame | Thin frame | Thick frame |
| Tend to be skinny | Moderate weight | Tend to be overweight |
| Dry hair | Soft, oily hair | Thick, wavy hair |
| Small eyes | Penetrating eyes | Big, attractive eyes |
| Very active | Moderately active | Lethargic |
| Irregular sleep | Little but sound sleep | Heavy sleep |
| Variable appetite | Good appetite | Slow but steady appetite |
| Restless mind | Sharp intellect | Calm, slow mental activity |

qualities listed above which apply to you.  Some people very clearly fall into one of these three categories.  Others exhibit combinations of these traits.  Looking at these charts, we can see that we cannot always take a person at "face value," nor should we be quick to judge others according to physical attributes.  Surface differences don't necessarily reveal the important qualities of the person inside.

How comfortable are you with physical differences?  Have you ever avoided greeting someone because of his or her physical dissimilarity from you?  Was it because you thought that person might be unable to communicate, or perhaps because you were uncomfortable about the difference itself?  Describe your reaction.

_____

_____

_____

Sometimes children are embarrassed or even frightened when they encounter a physical difference.  They might feel vulnerable, believing that a disability is contagious.  They may behave self-consciously, not knowing how they should act, or how the person with disabilities will act.  They may be worried that something strange might happen.  What other reactions might you expect?

_____

_____

Children may be curious, wondering what caused the disability, how the person functions, and what it would feel like to live with a disability (Berry, 1996).

Clearly, having children with physical differences in the classroom compels the teacher to help all the students to overcome ignorance and fear. Negative, destructive attitudes cause some children to exclude others from groups and learning experiences, thereby depriving everyone of enriching relationships.

> **VOICES OF EXPERIENCE**
>
> *"Example is not the main thing in influencing others.  It is the only thing."*
> —*Dr. Albert Schweitzer, Alsatian missionary*

Thomas Bergman (1989), a Swedish advocate for children with disabilities, points out that we, ourselves, set up social barriers which turn those with disabilities into handicapped people.  Can you think of some examples of how this happens every day?  Write your ideas below:

_____

_____

_____

When people who use wheelchairs must sit at the bottom of a step to a library or a theater, or those needing crutches or canes must walk where there is snow or ice, then they are handicapped (Bergman, 1989).

As a society, we have realized that people who have disabilities need the opportunity to develop to their fullest potential.  What do you consider our best hope for positive change in the years to come?

_____

_____

As with the discrimination we have discussed in earlier chapters, our best hope for positive change lies in educating our children about physical differences. We must foster in ourselves and in our students the idea that "respect for what people can do [must] take the place of pity for what they cannot do" (Bergman, 1989, p. 7).

PERSPECTIVE
TWO

Body size is obviously variable, but children whose size significantly varies from the average still may find themselves isolated physically and emotionally.  Those who are obese, or are unusually thin, small, or tall may be subject to harassment or discrimination because of physical differences.  It is important to educate yourself about some causes of these physical differences.

> ### Spotlight
> #### on the Classroom
>
> *"Imagine wearing a sign on your forehead that reads, 'I was an abused child,' or 'I have problems with my boyfriend,' or even 'I am afraid of the dark.'  Your classmates would stare at you and make snide remarks.  They might laugh as you walk by.  The luxury of those problems is that they can be hidden in your mind, and the note on your forehead doesn't really exist.*
>
> *"People who are overweight wear their problem on the outside, for all the world to see.  Fat. It's a three letter word that I am pretty familiar with.  I am not looking for sympathy, but if losing weight were easy I would have done it by now.*
>
> *"I want the world to realize that I know I am overweight.  Don't censor conversation in the classroom when I walk in.  Don't avoid sharing your bag of potato chips!  Let me make my own choices, and when I am ready, if I am ready, then I will take on the task of losing weight."*
> —Tracy A., student

Approximately 38 million Americans are significantly heavier than average (National Association to Advance Fat Acceptance, 1995). How are people who are obese discriminated against?

_____

_____

People who are obese are discriminated against in education, employment, and access to medical care and to public accommodations. They are the victims of cruel and tasteless jokes and constant assaults on their dignity.

Most weight problems appear to be hereditary. Scientists have recently isolated a "fat gene" which could genetically predispose a person to be overweight. More and more doctors are now advocating a stable weight, sensible diet, and exercise for fitness rather than equating thinness with health. In any case, stereotyping children by body weight and attaching a stigma to size is clearly an act of ignorance as well as one of cruelty.

> **VOICES OF EXPERIENCE**
>
> *We never know how*
> *    high we are*
> *Till we are called to rise*
> *And then, if we are*
> *    true to plan*
> *Our statures touch the*
> *    skies*
> *—Emily Dickinson,*
> *American poet*

Thinness, like obesity, may be associated with an individual's metabolism rather than with an eating disorder. Some people may be genetically predisposed to thinness. Anorexia, a lack of appetite and/or inability to eat, is a specific disease. Labels such as "anorexic" should never be used by anyone except a trained diagnostician.

The pituitary gland releases growth hormones which stimulate cell reproduction and help to increase body growth. Deficiencies or excesses of growth hormone in childhood can cause extreme variations in a person's height. Oversecretion of growth hormone, usually caused by a pituitary tumor, results in *gigantism*. An individual with gigantism may reach a height of seven to eight feet. Height which is below the fifth percentile on an incremental chart is called *dwarfism*. The causes of dwarfism can be environmental or genetic. Today, genetically engineered growth hormones can be periodically injected in children to spur their growth.

If you or your students find any of these physical differences difficult to encounter, or have been affected by the stereotypes portrayed in movies and television, remember that thinness as an ideal is very recent in history. Extra weight was thought of as a sign of affluence and health in the last century, and women were thought of as voluptuous rather than "fat." Keep in mind that a basketball player whose height is more than 7 feet is considered a star, not an exception, and an Olympic gymnast who is four and one-half feet tall is not a subject of ridicule for his or her difference. Jockeys are prized for their small size and are paid very well for being "different." When you notice a physical difference, whether it is one of size or stature, remember to look at the person instead of the difference.

Think of some ways in which our society thoughtlessly discriminates on the basis of size and stature. Name a few examples below:

_____

_____

_____

Desks and chairs in classrooms often are designed only for "average" height and weight. Water fountains, toilets, sinks, and doorways in schools are also built for the needs of the "average" student.

PERSPECTIVE
THREE

Why is a policy of inclusion and understanding of personal interest to each of us?

_____

_____

_____

_____

At some point in our lives, most of us will have to cope with a physical disability. Physical disabilities are problems caused by injuries or conditions of the central nervous system which interfere with mobility, coordination, communication, or behavior. Orthopedic impairments may be caused by such congenital abnormalities as clubfoot or absence of a limb, or by impairments such as cerebral palsy, amputations, burns, and fractures. As we age, many of us suffer disabling conditions such as arthritis, and one in every twenty babies is *born* with some type of disability. Therefore, when we think of the necessity of providing access and support to "people with disabilities" in our schools, we are most likely thinking of ourselves and our families.

Familiarize yourself with the following terminology relating to common physical differences.

**Acquired disability.** This is a condition resulting from illness or injury.

**Arthritis.** This is a painful disease which restricts movement of the joints.

**Atrophy.** This refers to a wasting away of muscles which are unused, such as after an injury.

**Brain damage.** This refers to a brain defect which prevents certain movement or affects thought, vision, or hearing.

**Cerebral Palsy.** This is a non progressive disorder of movement or posture that begins in childhood and is caused by a malfunctioning of or damage to the brain.

**Congenital disability.** This is a condition a person has from birth which limits ability.

**Hemiplegia.** This refers to paralysis of one side of the body.

**Impairment.** This is a loss of strength, feeling, or ability to move.

**Monoplegia.** This refers to paralysis of one extremity.

**Multiple sclerosis.** This is a degenerative, progressive disease of the central nervous system which involves hardening of the brain tissue. The symptoms include weak muscles, spasticity, balance difficulties, severe numbness of the appendages, and paraplegia. Symptoms may have periods of remission.

**Muscular Dystrophy.** This is an inherited condition resulting in progressive weakening and deteriorating of muscular tissue.

**Orthopedic.** This has to do with the bones, muscles, and joints used in movement.

**Paraplegia.** This refers to paralysis of the lower part of the body, usually caused by damage to the spinal cord.

**Physical disability in schools.** This refers to a physical impairment which is significant and chronic such that the child needs special care or education in order to be successful with learning.

**Physical therapy.** This method of treating a disability or injury may involve exercise, massage, medication, and education.

**Prosthesis.** This is an artificial replacement for a missing body part, such as an arm, hand, or leg.

**Quadriplegia.** This refers to paralysis of the body from the neck down.

**Spasticity.** This refers to sudden muscle contractions that a person cannot control.

**Spina Bifida.** This is a congenital disorder which causes an opening of the spinal column in the lower back. It is the most common birth defect in North America and is the major cause of paraplegia in young children (Ward, 1988).

EMPOWERMENT
TIPS

Following are some suggestions that will empower you to deal effectively with physical differences.

- *Treat all children alike.* Do not refer to those smaller in stature as "cute" or "shorty," and don't expect more mature behavior from a child of above average height for his or her age.

- *Extend your hand first when you are being introduced to anyone.* Make eye contact. Failure to do so excludes those with disabilities or differences.

- *Respect wheelchairs as part of the user's space.* Don't assume that he or she wishes to be moved. Always ask whether your assistance is needed.

- *Be an attentive listener to children who have a disability.* Never pretend to understand. Ask them to repeat when necessary.

- *Put yourself in the line of sight of the child to whom you are speaking.* Don't force someone in a wheelchair to strain in order to see you.

- *Never use labels to describe anyone.* The disability is not the person and should never be used to describe him or her.

- *Do not hesitate to touch children with disabilities.* Interact with them naturally as with all students.

98

Use the following classroom strategies to foster your students' understanding of the implications of physical differences.

- Plan and carry out with your class an imaginary trip around your school, your town, or a favorite place such as a park or stadium. Make a list together of all the places you would not have been able to go in a wheelchair (note curbs, narrow doors, stairs, stares, and other impediments).

- Explain to your students exactly what it means to say that someone has a physical disability. "Having a physical disability restricts the way people can move their bodies. Some people with physical disabilities cannot walk well and some cannot walk at all. Some people cannot control any part of their body. Some people cannot control the movements of their muscles" (Bergman, 1989, p. 42).

- Have students ask their parents whether there were curb cuts when they were children and whether there were ramps at school so kids and teachers in wheelchairs could get in the school.

- Explain to your students that people who use wheelchairs don't stay in them all the time. "A wheelchair is a way of getting around, like a car or a bike. Unless people need to be kept in wheelchairs for their own safety, they can sit on chairs or couches when they want to. Some people who use wheelchairs can walk, too, but are not able to all the time" (Bergman, 1989, p. 43).

- Have the class check newspaper and magazine reviews and ads for restaurants and theaters to see if there is information about wheelchair accessibility.

- Talk specifically about the causes of particular disabilities. Information dispels fear as it educates, and allows students to relinquish stereotypes.

- Discuss the fact that the word *spastic* comes from the word *spasm* and means a sudden, uncontrollable muscle contraction. When the word is misused to insult a friend, it makes people who are disabled feel uncomfortable and unwanted (Bergman, 1989).

- Conduct an activity that examines which physical attributes are portrayed as typical within society. Allow students to investigate and then guide a group discussion about how accurate the so-called typical attributes are.

Finally, let's return to the scenario that opened this chapter. Read the situation below and record your reactions. Answering the questions will prepare you to handle physical differences in the classroom. There is no one "right" answer.

Setting: Your classroom
Time: Just after class convenes
Persons involved: Your students and their parents
Background: You have been out sick for a day. Mr. Sanchez, your substitute, uses a wheelchair.
Circumstances: Upon your return, you find that the students had reacted in a generally negative way toward Mr. Sanchez. Several parents have expressed their dismay at his being in the classroom.
Simulation: Susan, a leader and opinion-maker in your class, greets you with "We're so glad you're back. Mr. Sanchez was weird. We didn't know what to say to him. My mother says cripples shouldn't be allowed to teach."

1. What are your objectives?

_____

_____

_____

2. What do you plan to say to the parents?

_____

_____

_____

3. What do you say to the students?

_____

_____

_____

4. What will you say to Mr. Sanchez?

_____

_____

_____

5. How might you foster a better reaction in the future?

_____

_____

_____

CONCLUSION    When your students meet someone who uses a wheelchair, an individual with a prosthetic arm or leg, a person who is missing a limb, or an individual whose body is scarred due to a severe burn, challenge them to see beyond that person's difference. Whether different due to body size or disability, that person deserves respect. If your students' individual comfort levels seem to be affected by physical differences, take steps to have them interact more often with persons who look different. Your students will discover that the "difference" will fade away.

REFERENCES    Bergman, T. (1989). *On our own terms: Children living with physical disabilities.* Milwaukee: Gareth Stevens Children's Books.

Berry, J. (1996). *Good answers to tough questions about physical disabilities.* Chicago: Children's Press.

National Association to Advance Fat Acceptance. (1995). *Fighting size discrimination and prejudice.* Sacramento, CA: Author.

Ward, B. R. (1988). *Overcoming disability.* London: Franklin Watts.

# Learning Differences in the Classroom

OBJECTIVES    By the end of this chapter you should be able to answer these questions:

- What is the primary way learning disabilities are identified?
- What is one characteristic shared by all students with learning disabilities?
- What are four possible causes of learning disabilities?
- What are five specific types of learning disabilities?
- What are six strategies for assisting someone with a learning disability?

THE CLASSROOM IS A MICROCOSM

*During your school's open house, parents drop by for informal chats. The mother of Stanley Chester, one of your pupils with a learning disability, sits down to talk with you. Mrs. Chester indicates that Stanley hates school. She says she doesn't blame him because many of his classmates insult him by calling him "stupid" and "retard" since he uses a tape recorder in lieu of writing notes in class. She also tells you that Stanley's siblings make fun of him because of his difficulty with homework. You mention the fact that Stanley's spotty attendance isn't helping his grades. "I let him stay home on days when he doesn't feel up to the teasing," Mrs. Chester admits. "He really does feel sick from it, you know."*

INTRODUCTION

When you learn a new game, what do you do first—read all the rules, watch others play, or just start playing and learn as you go? When you are introduced to new information, do you remember it better if you see it on paper, hear it, write it, or say it aloud? No two people learn in exactly the same way. Students with learning differences may be good at processing information in one way but not in another.

We frequently rely upon technological aids to make learning easier. Name below a

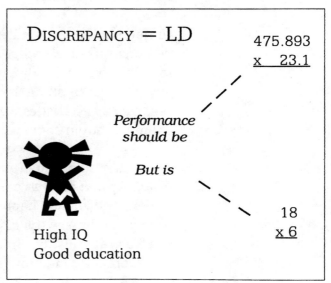

DISCREPANCY = LD

$$475.893 \times 23.1$$

*Performance should be*

*But is*

High IQ
Good education

$$18 \times 6$$

few such devices you use:

_____

_____

We often use calculators for difficult math calculations, word processors to check our grammar and spelling, and tape recorders to record or play back information. Books on tape often sell as well as their printed counterparts. Computer programs help us to master foreign languages, learn to draw, and balance our checkbooks. Clearly, many of us take advantage of ways to augment our learning. And many teachers and their students are underachievers, whether academically or professionally. Students with learning disabilities, though, may not have poor achievement because they have learned good coping strategies. Learning disabilities can be related to disorders of thinking, learning, and sometimes of communication. They are called by different names, and there are many types, but we will use the general term *learning disability* to describe the exceptionality in general, and briefly discuss a few of the specific types in more detail.

A learning disability is an invisible disability. Because students with learning disabilities are in the normal range of intelligence and may function perfectly well in certain contexts, it is sometimes difficult to assess their problem. Students with learning disabilities look and act like everyone else for the most part. When might the disability become apparent?

_____

_____

Until a student is asked to read, write, solve mathematical problems or demonstrate some other academic skill, or until he or she exhibits the inability to organize learning tasks, it may not be apparent that there is any problem at all. A student with a learning difference may be able to recite sports statistics, remember song lyrics, or show artistic talent, for example, but in some particular areas be unable to perform adequately.

It may be frustrating for both the student with a learning disability and for that person's family, friends, and teachers to understand what is happening and to cope with the problem, especially until such time as the difficulty is properly diagnosed. The reason for the frustration is that frequently the student with a learning disability has average to high intelligence and cognitive ability. This chapter seeks to introduce the many facets of learning disabilities so that you will be better equipped to understand your students who learn differently.

Students with learning differences are frequently successful because they have developed techniques for camouflaging their differences and getting by in the world. Many of your colleagues and associates likely have learning differences, though you may be unaware of it. For example, a business executive who has trouble reading or writing might dictate letters and have a secretary type them. In this case, the potential disability is circumvented. Another person might rely upon digital watches to tell the time, or calculators to solve math problems. Such a person can accurately tell time and solve math problems by using assistive technology. A traveler lost on the road might ask for directions rather than consult a map, again taking advantage of other sources of information. Someone may even pretend to read a book or newspaper while sitting on the city bus in an effort to fit in with the crowd. Indeed, an entire culture of learning has arisen to aid people with learning differences in succeeding in life and going unnoticed.

> **VOICES OF EXPERIENCE**
>
> *"Learning is but an adjunct to ourself."*
> *—William Shakespeare, playwright*

Learning disabilities are the newest categories of exceptionality, having been identified only since the 1960s by educators and parent groups. Estimates of the number of students with learning disabilities range from 15 to 50 percent. Many students are not diagnosed with learning disabilities until college level. Have you ever had trouble following a lecture, understanding a reading assignment, or keeping up with the pace of a classroom activity? Explain below:

_____

_____

_____

_____

Three to five percent of college students are diagnosed with learning disabilities, even though they experienced no difficulties in their earlier school experiences. It has been estimated that over one million children will have received stimulant medication in the 1990s in attempts to treat learning disorders (Associated Press News Service, 1989). Of all categories of exceptionality, learning disability (LD) affects the greatest number of individuals and requires the greatest number of instructional personnel. It also is the subject of the most disagreement about definition and diagnosis, as well as treatment methods and educational services.

Some exceptionalities, such as race, gender, physical disability, size, or age, for example, are obvious because of their characteristic features or behaviors. Why are learning disabilities so difficult to identify?

_____

_____

_____

_____

Learning disabilities are very difficult to identify because students with LD are more like those without it than not. There is an extremely broad range of problems associated with learning disability, and its effect varies in degree from very mild to severe. The primary way that the exceptionality of LD is identified is by comparing a student to other students in his or her age bracket to determine if there is a discrepancy between expected achievement and actual performance. This discrepancy model is the basic method for identifying a student with a learning disability. For example, if an eight-year-old girl is not performing at the average or expected level for her age, IQ, educational opportunity, and ability, her poor performance is most likely due to some sort of learning disability. The girl is also likely to be exhibiting some social or behavioral problems as a result of the way the LD affects her feelings and/or the responses of the people around her.

> ### Spotlight
> #### on the Classroom
>
> *"At age 14, Susan still tends to be quiet. Ever since she was a child, she was so withdrawn that people sometimes forgot she was there. She seemed to drift into a world of her own. When she did talk, she often called objects by the wrong names. She had few friends and mostly played with dolls or her little sister. In school, Susan hated reading and math because none of the letters, numbers or "+" and "-" signs made any sense. She felt awful about herself. She'd been told— and was convinced—that she was retarded. Susan was promoted to the sixth grade but still couldn't do basic math. So, her mother took her to a private clinic for testing. The clinician observed that Susan had trouble associating symbols with their meaning, and this was holding back her language, reading, and math development. Susan called objects by the wrong words and she could not associate sounds with letters or recognize math symbols. However, an IQ of 128 meant that Susan was quite bright. In addition to developing an Individualized Education Plan, the clinician recommended that Susan receive counseling for her low self-esteem and depression."*
> *—report from the National Institutes of Health (1993)*

Let's examine some generalities about learning disorders and disabilities. Traditionally, perception, memory, and attention have been areas of concern, and educators, doctors, and psychologists have all had their different ways of assessing and addressing the problems. For example, educators may use such terms as *specific learning disabilities*. Psychologists may talk about *perceptual disorders* and *hyperkinetic behavior*. Speech and language specialists use such terms as *aphasia* and *dyslexia*. Doctors may use such labels as *dysfunction*, *impairment*, or *brain injury*.

We can say as lay persons that individuals with LD have, at some point in their lives, all experienced poor achievement in some context, and that that poor achievement was associated with learning needs. What might be a damaging repercussion of this poor achievement?

_____

_____

Since performance and achievement affect self-concept, and learning disabilities may inhibit the development of social and interpersonal skills as well, often individuals with LD may suffer emotionally and socially, though this is not always the case.

The causes of learning disabilities are the subject of much examination and debate. Prenatal research shows that a mother's use of tobacco during pregnancy may have damaging effects on the unborn child (National Institutes of Health, 1993). Mothers who smoke during pregnancy are more likely to bear smaller babies. This is a concern because small newborns, especially those weighing less than 5 pounds, tend to be at risk for a variety of problems, including learning disorders.

Alcohol also may be dangerous to the baby's developing brain. It appears that alcohol may distort the developing neurons. Heavy alcohol consumption during pregnancy has been linked to Fetal Alcohol Syndrome, a condition that can lead to low birth weight, intellectual impairment, hyperactivity, and certain physical defects. Any alcohol use during pregnancy, however, may influence the child's development and lead to problems with learning, attention, memory, or problem solving.

Drugs such as cocaine—especially in its smokable form, "crack"—seem to affect the normal development of brain receptors. These specialized neural cells help to transmit incoming signals from our skin, eyes, and ears, and help to regulate our physical response to the environment. Because children with certain learning disabilities have trouble understanding speech sounds or letters, some researchers believe that LD may be related to faulty receptors. Current research points to drug abuse as a possible cause of receptor damage (National Institutes of Health, 1993).

Genetic abnormalities (passed on from parent to child) are another possible cause of learning disabilities. Complications during delivery, such as when the umbilical cord becomes twisted and temporarily cuts off oxygen to the baby, can also impair brain functions and lead to LD.

For a year or so after a child is born, fragile new brain cells and neural networks continue to be produced. Neuroscientists are identifying certain environmental toxins that may lead to learning disabilities, possibly by disrupting early childhood brain development or brain processes. Cadmium and lead, both prevalent in the environment, are becoming a leading focus of neurological research. Cadmium, used in making some steel products, can be carried from the soil into the foods we eat. Lead was once common in paint and gasoline—it is still present in some water pipes. A study of animals sponsored by the National Institutes of Health revealed a connection between exposure to lead and learning difficulties. In the study, rats exposed to lead experienced changes in their brainwaves, slowing their ability to learn. The learning problems lasted for weeks, long after the rats were no longer exposed to lead (National Institutes of Health, 1993).

Other environmental factors, including lack of reinforcement for learning by parents, radiation stress, fluorescent lighting, poor nutrition, food additives, and unshielded television tubes have been targeted as possible causes of LD. Clearly, learning disabilities have different causes, and any one disability may have many causes. Scientific research into this complex exceptionality is on-going, though no one factor has been proven conclusively.

PERSPECTIVE
THREE

Let's conduct an experiment of our own. Read the following paragraph quickly:

*Down syndrome si a disaes dezirertcarahc by wol
I.W., shrot and broad hands, and woleb average
thgieh. Ti is more birth DNA there is no crue.*

This is how an individual with a severe learning disability may see words. Did it take you longer than usual to read and understand it?

Imagine having to deal with all reading materials in this fashion.

Now quickly write your name and address in the space below, but write all of the words backwards:

_____

_____

Do you think people with learning disabilities feel the way you do now when faced with a difficult task?

_____

_____

PERSPECTIVE
FOUR

Clearly, not all learning problems are actual disabilities. There is a continuum of learning differences, ranging from general learning style preferences to specific neurological damage (YMCA, 1996):

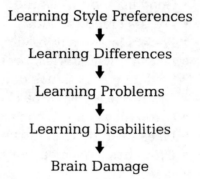

Learning Style Preferences
↓
Learning Differences
↓
Learning Problems
↓
Learning Disabilities
↓
Brain Damage

As a classroom teacher, you may not be able to diagnose exactly where each of your students falls on this learning continuum. And it may be difficult, if not impossible, to tailor your teaching methods to *every* student's learning style, difference, or disability. If a particular student seems to be having difficulties, arrange for a private tutor to work with that student one-to-one. Through observation, discussion, experimentation, and modeling, the tutor can assess how your student learns best and teach him or her how to study accordingly. It is easier for tutors to adjust the way they teach than it is for your students to change the way they learn (YMCA, 1996).

Though tutors are a valuable resource, all classroom teachers must be keenly aware of how their students learn. By noticing the strategies that your students use to process information and to solve problems, you can discover a great deal about how they think and learn

(YMCA, 1996).  There are three general categories of information processing: 1) visual, 2) auditory, and 3) tactile/kinesthetic.  Though each student combines these modes to some extent, one mode will usually dominate as the primary learning style.  Consider the following characteristics (derived from YMCA, 1996) as you observe your students' learning styles:

- Visual Learner
  - Scans everything; wants to see things; enjoys visual stimuli
  - Stores visual images
  - Enjoys shapes, colors, patterns, maps, pictures, diagrams
  - Can recall words after seeing them a few times
  - Has difficulty in lectures
  - Daydreams
  - Can vividly describe visual details of a scene
  - Often a good speller; internalizes spelling patterns quickly
  - Prefers written directions/notes
  - Often finds locations by landmarks

- Auditory Learner
  - Good listener; often the "talker"
  - Prefers oral directions
  - Prefers lectures to reading assignments
  - Likes to hear stories, poems, music
  - Seldom writes things down
  - Often repeats what has been said
  - Often moves lips while reading
  - Likes to study with music or the television on
  - Often has a good ear for music

- Tactile/Kinesthetic Learner
  - The "do-er"
  - Needs to touch, handle, manipulate materials and objects
  - Counts on fingers
  - Good at drawing designs
  - Often doodles while listening, especially on the telephone
  - Needs to get up and move around in order to process information
  - Good at sports, mechanics, using appliances, or tools
  - Often enjoys hiking, jogging, other non-stationary activities

An awareness of these basic learning styles will help you to adjust your expectations for individual students.  Always remember that all students are learning all the time—just in different ways.

Following are some broad, thumbnail definitions of a few categories of the exceptionality called learning disability. It is a good rule to be cautious about using these terms without the guidance of a professional. This list is offered solely for the purpose of introducing you to a few of the most commonly used terms.

**Aphasia.** Aphasia is the loss or impairment of the ability to use spoken or written language. A person experiencing aphasia may not be able to recall the name of a familiar person or object.

**Brain injury.** An individual with brain injury is described as having an organic impairment which results in perceptual problems, thinking disorders, and emotional instability (Hardman, Drew, Egan & Wolf, 1993).

**Dyscalculia.** Impairment in arithmetic or computation skills is called dyscalculia. People with dyscalculia may have trouble counting, writing numbers, or solving even simple addition or subtraction problems because they are unable to relate to the numerical figures.

**Dysgraphia.** Impairment in the ability to write is called dysgraphia. People with dysgraphia may know how to spell a word but be unable to write it on paper. They may also have difficulty with handwriting, word spacing, or letter formation, or they may write very slowly.

**Dyslexia.** Impairment in the ability to read is called dyslexia. People with dyslexia may have trouble spelling certain words and may invert letters of the alphabet. They may also have difficulty with comprehension as a side-effect of the dyslexia.

**Hyperactivity.** This is a behavioral characteristic which is also often termed *hyperkinetic.* Hyperactivity is typically a general excess of activity. Individuals may be described as fidgety, nervous, or distractible.

**Minimal brain dysfunction.** This classification has become outdated, but you may still come across it occasionally. A person who shows behavioral but not neurological signs of brain damage is sometimes diagnosed with "minimal brain dysfunction" or "minimal brain injury." People with minimal brain dysfunction are often average or above average in intelligence.

**Perception disorders.** Perception problems for individuals with LD may include a wide range of difficulties, including visual, auditory, and haptic (touch, body movement) sensory systems. Visual and auditory difficulties in LD should not be confused with the characteristics associated with hearing and vision exceptionalities. These perceptual problems are entirely different. They have to do with perception, rather than with hearing and vision, per se. An example would be clearly seeing a word on paper yet reversing the order of letters.

**Specific learning disability.** A legal definition which has been incorporated into federal law is that specific learning disability is a "disorder in one or more of the basic psychological processes involved in understanding or in using language, spoken or written, which may manifest itself in an imperfect ability to listen, think, speak, read, write, spell, or to do mathematical calculations" (Individuals with Disabilities Education Act, 1990).

EMPOWERMENT
TIPS

Following are some suggestions that will empower you to deal effectively with people who learn differently.

❧ *Live by these rules of thumb* (adapted from Poor Richard, 1996):

- Pull as much as you can out of those around you.
- Extend yourself.
- Be creative.
- Don't assess someone's capabilities based on IQ scores.
- Don't be afraid to make mistakes in front of others. If learning takes place through modeling, you must model the process of working things out, from scratch, mistakes and all.
- Assume that others are always doing their best.
- Remember that we all learn differently.

❧ *Learn about advocacy groups which provide information about learning disabilities.* These groups will provide support for your students with learning disabilities and their families, and can keep you up to date on LD research.

❧ *Act to secure treatment and protective legislation for those with LD.* Offer your help and support.

❧ *Volunteer as a tutor for children or adults with learning disabilities.* Many organizations provide training for volunteers at no cost.

❧ *Promote the development of functional academic programs for LD students in your local schools.* Talk to school personnel to determine what programs are currently being offered for LD students, and suggest the development of a program if necessary.

❧ *Establish eye contact before giving or repeating instructions.* Establishing eye contact helps to make a stronger connection between you and the person with whom you are communicating.

- *It is important to be patient and to remember that the difficulties of individuals with LD do not come from lack of motivation or intelligence.* Think of the problem as a challenge to you to communicate more clearly.

- *Encourage persons with LD to seek assistance from agencies which offer special help.* Newspapers, talking books, and many other services are available in most communities.

- *Encourage a positive attitude toward the exceptionality of LD among your friends, family, neighbors, and students.* They, like you, will certainly encounter and interact with many people in their lives who have learning disabilities. The information you share may help them to identify their own LD in some cases, as well.

CLASSROOM STRATEGIES

Here are a number of concrete strategies you can use in the classroom to help minimize learning problems:

- When you experience a problem, or see a problem that a student with LD is having, focus on the environment rather than on the learner. For instance, try to express directions more clearly, or in another way, or try demonstrating instead of telling the instructions.

- Do not give students too much information at one time. Present instructions or information in small increments, so that the students are not overwhelmed. Consider listing the day's activities and assignments on the chalkboard each day. This will give students an overall picture of what to expect.

- Model the behavior you desire or are trying to teach. Modeling is much more effective than telling, either in speech or in writing. Ignore inappropriate behavior whenever possible, and reward and reinforce positive or appropriate behavior. Whatever you put your attention on will increase and grow, so why not put your attention on positive behavior?

- Allow students with learning disabilities to use assistive technology in the classroom (tape recorders, spelling computers, calculators, and so on). If other students complain, explain that these devices are not "special favors" but important tools, just as eyeglasses are tools that help people to see better and hearing aids are tools that help people to hear better. Remember that accommodations are required by the Individuals with Disabilities Education Act.

● Write down information when possible. Check to be sure your students understand the instructions. Always review information. It is helpful to repeat frequently, so that learning is reinforced.

● Teach your students that the following stereotypes about people with learning differences are *not* true:

- They can't understand
- They represent a small minority
- They are not trying hard enough
- They all have brain damage
- They are "slow"
- They always have trouble academically
- They cannot read or write
- Their social and emotional well-being is not affected
- They usually outgrow their learning disabilities
- They need special classes
- Teachers can always identify children with learning disabilities

● Use the following strategies for visual learners (derived from YMCA, 1996):

- Associate sounds with pictures (b - bird)
- Use colored markers to highlight word parts
- Use colored markers to emphasize punctuation
- Assist student in creating meaningful visual cues for memory
- Explain how to do a problem/activity by demonstrating in writing
- Encourage students to draw pictures and label parts
- Use games and puzzles when possible
- Always include written directions with assignments
- Use pictures or graphs to organize readings or writings

● Use the following strategies for auditory learners (derived from YMCA, 1996):

- Give directions orally first
- Ask students to repeat what was heard
- Allow students to give oral as well as written reports
- Encourage students to sub-vocalize (read under breath)
- Discuss a story both before and after reading it
- Use a tape recorder as a learning tool
- Encourage student to spell and work out math problems aloud
- Use mnemonic aids for memory
- Teach students to "talk themselves through" assignments
- Read stories aloud

🍎 Use the following strategies for tactile/kinesthetic learners (derived from YMCA, 1996):

- Use touchable materials whenever possible (measuring cups, checkbooks, rulers, abacus, and so on)
- Allow for independent work on a computer—use of the keyboard and mouse are highly tactile
- Have students trace over letters and numbers; cut out sandpaper letters for extra stimulation
- Use a moveable alphabet to practice spelling
- Make sure student watches you make sounds and watches as you give directions
- Encourage lip reading and following along with finger
- Use charades to demonstrate lessons or give directions
- Visit sites whenever possible (e.g. go to the bank to fill out forms, cook in a kitchen, etc.)

🍎 Share the following advice with your students (derived from Poor Richard, 1996):

- Consider everything an experiment.
- Learn by trial and error, and don't avoid the errors.
- Learning doesn't happen in class, it happens when you get home and look at the wall. Don't forget to set aside time for looking at walls.
- Be self-disciplined.
- Be a self-advocate.
- Learn from your mistakes. There is no win and no fail, there's only honest effort.
- Assume that others are always doing their best.
- Get good at something other than school-related work (like skateboarding or cooking).
- Don't try to create and analyze at the same time. They're different processes.
- Don't spend energy worrying; just get started and potential difficulties will work out.
- Subscribe to lots of magazines, the more pictures the better. Don't feel bad about not reading them cover to cover—just have them around and read what interests you, even if it's just one article.
- It's the process, not the product, that counts, because you can use it again and again and it transfers.
- Avoid doing school-related work under pressure. Always allow lots of extra time for things that are difficult, and for everything else, too.
- Learning opportunities are everywhere, not just in academic settings. The more stuff you do, the more you learn.

- Read anything you can get your hands on. Comic books involve decoding just as great literature does. Read billboards and road signs.
- Write lots of letters.
- Look at movies carefully, often.
- Learn to ask questions without feeling stupid.
- Travel whenever and wherever you can.
- Give others some slack; it makes life easier.
- Give yourself some slack; it makes life easier.

CLASSROOM SIMULATION Finally, let's return to the scenario that opened this chapter. Read the situation below and record your reactions. Answering the questions will prepare you to handle learning differences in the classroom. There is no one "right" answer.

| | |
|---|---|
| Setting: | Your classroom |
| Time: | Mid-afternoon |
| Persons involved: | The mother of Stanley Chester |
| Background: | Stanley is a student who exhibits a learning disability |
| Circumstances: | You are meeting Stanley's mother for a casual conversation during open house. |
| Simulation: | Mrs. Chester indicates that Stanley hates school. She doesn't blame him because many of his classmates insult him because he uses a tape recorder to take notes. Mrs. Chester says that she allows Stanley to miss class frequently because he feels physically sick from the teasing. |

1. What do you want to accomplish as you talk with Mrs. Chester?

_____

_____

_____

2. What will you suggest to Mrs. Chester about Stanley's absences?

_____

_____

_____

3. What suggestions will you make regarding Stanley's classmates?

_____

_____

_____

4. What will you say to your class the next day?

_____

_____

_____

5. How might you prevent such an occurrence from happening again?

_____

_____

_____

CONCLUSION     This chapter has introduced an exceptionality which is complex and comprehensive, and so offers you special challenges. You have seen that the term *learning disabilities* is broad and generic and that it involves different specific problems. The study of this exceptionality is relatively new, and though a variety of disciplines such as medicine, education, and psychology have undertaken it, even the conceptual development and terminology related to LD are still in the formative stages. The field is growing at a rapid pace, and our understanding is increasing. At the present time we can say only that those individuals exhibiting the characteristics of learning disabilities are so varied that we cannot describe them with any one concept or term.

Meanwhile, educators have developed excellent interventions for students with learning disabilities. "Learning Strategies," developed by researchers at the University of Kansas, have become recognized for their ability to assist persons with LD to *learn how to learn*. Special educators, who are trained in Learning Strategies, have seen significant improvements among students with learning disabilities as the strategies have provided structured ways for these students to learn effectively.

One major problem with people who live with learning disabilities is not their skills but their self-concept. It's difficult to advance when you are constantly thinking that you are not as good as everyone else. A classroom teacher's ultimate responsibility is to dispel lowered expectations from students' minds.

REFERENCES    Associated Press News Service. (1989, June 3). 750,000 children take stimulants researchers say.

Hardman, M., Drew, C., Egan, M., & Wolf, B. (1993). *Human exceptionality: Society, school, and family* (4th ed.). Boston: Allyn and Bacon.

Individuals with Disabilities Education Act. (1990). Washington, DC: U.S. Government Printing Office.

National Institutes of Health. (1993). Learning disabilities: Decade of the brain. [On-line.] Available: gopher://zippy.nimh.nih.gov:70/00/documents/nimh/other/learn

Poor Richard's Publishing. (1996). Tips and advice for students, teachers, and parents. In *Poor Richard's publishing home page.* [On-line.] Available: http://www.tiac.net/users/poorrich/tipsadvice.html

YMCA. (1996). Tutor tips: Learning differences and disabilities. In *Adult literacy homepage.* [On-line.] Available: http://libertynet.org/~ymcalit/lrndis.html

# Intellectual Diversity in the Classroom

OBJECTIVES

By the end of this chapter you should be able to answer these questions:

- How is intelligence defined?
- How is intelligence measured?
- Why are intelligence assessments controversial?
- What are ten qualities associated with advanced intellectual ability?
- What are the three criteria used to identify developmental delays?

THE CLASSROOM IS A MICROCOSM

*Linda Wan is one of your students who exhibits a developmental delay. After two years in special education classes, she now attends regular classes. She is fun-loving, enthusiastic about learning, shows promise as an athlete, and is a talented artist. However, Linda has seemed to be quite depressed lately. You've observed that she has not smiled once in class during the last week. She walks into your classroom to return a book she had borrowed. You say, "Linda, you've looked pretty down lately. What's the problem?" She answers, "I just wish they'd leave me alone. Why aren't I like everyone else? Why do all the kids call me 'retard'?"*

INTRODUCTION

Of all the differences we can observe between ourselves and others, perhaps the most important and the most interesting is intellectual difference. We use the terms *intellect* or *intelligence* to describe cognitive power—that is, the ability to learn and to process information. The classroom is an obvious center of learning and information processing, where students' intellectual abilities are constantly evaluated and challenged in oral discussions and written examinations.

We attempt to measure intelligence in many ways, including tests of creative thinking, verbal aptitude, academic knowledge, and psycho-motor skills. There continues to be disagreement among experts as to the validity and use of these tests, but they are in general use for

Curiosity, flexibility, talents, empathy, verbal skills, interest, originality, appreciation, vocabulary, persistence, concentration, memory, judgment, logic, leadership ability, artistic talents, creativity, ability

121

assessment of special needs and for placement in schools and programs.

It is a mistake to categorize students solely on the basis of an intelligence assessment. Name a reason why such a test may be misleading or unreliable:

_____

_____

Human beings have complex and surprising brains, and each of us has a broad range of aptitudes and potentialities. A test score alone can neither predict nor account for an individual's hidden potentials and abilities. At the extreme ends of assessment scales, however, are the exceptionalities of giftedness and mental retardation. Giftedness describes advanced abilities, while being developmentally delayed (often called *mental retardation*) describes limited intellectual abilities.

In order to establish norms for intelligence, researchers test random samples of populations which represent different ages, cultures, ethnicities, and genders. These studies are used to set a standard score, or norm. Individuals can then be compared to the norming group. You have no doubt taken any number of such tests during your school career: the G.R.E., S.A.T., A.C.T., and so on.

Society's definition of intelligence is not static. Through time, we have seen that many individuals realize potential achievement which is never indicated by any assessment scale. We also observe that many of us fail to perform at levels indicated as our potential. As we are able to see the truth that every human being has innate intelligence and therefore has value, we begin more and more to look for ways to enhance each person's potential.

Intelligence testing requires specialized training and is usually done by psychologists or others who are certified to administer the tests. Results of intelligence tests can be affected by cultural differences and other variables. Therefore, these results should always be understood in a limited context. They are designed to indicate areas in which a student might most benefit from specific instruction, for example.

The Wechsler Intelligence Scale for Children and the Stanford-Binet Intelligence Test are typically given to evaluate intellectual and developmental levels. Consider a time when you were tested, whether it was an intelligence or aptitude test, or a school exam. Did you feel that the test score or grade was a true indicator of your knowledge? Why or why not?

_____

_____

_____

Did you feel that the score was a true indicator of your *potential*? Why or why not?

_____

_____

_____

PERSPECTIVE
ONE

One of the best arguments for studying human diversity is the definition we give to giftedness. Below is a list of qualities associated with advanced intellect. Underline all that apply to you:

- Curiosity
- Flexibility
- Leadership ability
- Artistic talents
- Unusual empathy and concern for people
- Excellent verbal skills
- Genuine interest in learning
- Ability to grasp ideas
- Originality in thought
- Interest in designing, developing, and creating
- Ability to appreciate beauty
- Large vocabulary
- Persistence
- Ability to concentrate for long periods
- Read often
- Good memory
- Good judgment and logic

You can see that many of these qualities which we associate with giftedness indicate openness, multiple interests, and, in fact, diversity. Those who contribute most to our society are the ones who are themselves a celebration of diversity. Your classroom is like a petri dish,

123

swarming with living diversity, electrified with different impulses of intelligence.

Educators often define giftedness in terms of a high intelligence test score—typically two standard deviations above the mean—on individual or group measures. Parents and teachers alike usually recognize students with general intellectual talent by their expansive fund of general information, productive thinking, and high levels of vocabulary, memory, abstract word knowledge, and abstract reasoning (Gifted Resources, 1996). Using a broad definition of giftedness, a school system could expect to identify 10% to 15% of its student population as gifted and talented (Gifted Resources, 1996).

Indeed, the world abounds with examples of gifted, creative people. Gifted people in politics and business include Jesse Jackson, George Bush, Bill Clinton, Bill Gates, and Michael Eisner. Many of the most outstanding minds in history were not recognized for their abilities until they were older. For instance, Walt Disney was fired from a job because he had "no good ideas," and Winston Churchill failed sixth grade.

We label and use stereotypes for intellectual differences the same way we do for physical, racial, cultural, ethnic, and sexual orientation. What labels have been applied to you in regard to your intelligence? List a few below:

_____

_____

Most of us have been called "stupid" or "idiot" at one time or another. If you have been an honor student, you have probably been called "smart," "a brain," "genius," or even some negative term like "nerd" or "know-it-all." Sometimes those who are intellectually advanced are ostracized by classmates because they are different. The "gifted underachiever" phenomenon refers to highly talented students with poor academic performance, due perhaps to boredom, alienation, or the general feeling of being misplaced and misunderstood.

PERSPECTIVE
TWO

It is always a mistake to generalize about individuals. Students with limited intellectual ability, for example, do not fit stereotypes any more than do any other group. Developmental delay is a generic expression applied to physical or mental disabilities occurring before adulthood. This label is generally preferable to "mental retardation" or "mental handicap" because it does not convey the same negative connotations. A developmental delay is not a disease. Students exhibiting developmental delays do learn, but often slowly and with difficulty. Like any other students, they have the capacity to learn, to develop, and to grow.

According to a new definition by the American Association on Mental Retardation, adopted in 1992, an individual is considered to have mental retardation based on the following three criteria: 1) an intellectual functioning level (I.Q.) below 70-75; 2) significant limitations in two or more adaptive skill areas (those daily living skills needed to live, work and play in the community, including communication, self-care, home living, social skills, leisure, health and safety, self-direction, functional academics, community use and work); and 3) the condition being present from age 18 or earlier (New Bedford Harbor, 1996).

Characteristics of students with developmental delays can include:

- Language ability below their age group
- Play interests that are immature for their age
- Difficulty in generalizing
- Poor attention span
- Poor sensory skills
- Poor motor coordination
- Low frustration level
- Poor social skills
- Poor self-concepts
- Need to hear things many times to learn them
- Need to repeat activities many times to understand them

Numerous studies have been conducted in local communities to determine the prevalence of developmental delays. The Arc (formerly the Association of Retarded Citizens) concluded in 1982 that 2.5 to 3 percent of the general population has mental retardation. A 1993 review of prevalence studies generally confirmed this distribution (New Bedford Harbor, 1996). Based on the 1990 census, an estimated 6.2 to 7.5 million people have mental retardation, which means that one out of ten American families is directly affected by mental retardation (New Bedford Harbor, 1996).

Norman Alessi (1992), an expert on developmental delays and mental retardation, suggests that emotional and behavioral disorders are a frequent complication of developmental delays and may interfere with the child's progress. Alessi notes that "Most retarded children recognize that they are behind others of their own age. Some may become frustrated, withdrawn or anxious, or act 'bad' to get the attention of other youngsters and adults" (1992, p. 1). Children with developmental

125

delays may also become depressed. Without enough language skills to talk about their feelings, their depression may express itself through new problems in behavior, eating, and sleeping (Alessi, 1992).

Causes of developmental delays fall into five basic categories: genetic, prenatal, perinatal, postnatal, and psychosocial. We will examine each of these briefly.

Genetic causation typically manifests itself as Down Syndrome or Phenylketonuria (PKU). Down Syndrome is caused by a chromosomal abnormality which occurs in about one of every one-thousand births. PKU is a hereditary condition involving the absence of an enzyme essential to protein ingestion, causing toxicity in the brain. PKU, if detected early enough, can be controlled by diet and therefore not cause a developmental delay.

The unborn baby is vulnerable to certain diseases and traumas. Prenatal causation has been linked to Rubella, Syphilis, RH factor, Fetal Alcohol Syndrome, and drug addiction.

The actual birth itself is not without dangers. Perinatal causation has been traced to asphyxia, positioning, prolonged labor, and forceps delivery.

The developing child is vulnerable to accidents, environmental toxicity, and illnesses. Thus, postnatal causation includes injuries, brain tumors, lead poisoning, and high fevers (such as meningitis or encephalitis).

Finally, psychosocial causation includes malnutrition, the environment, poor infant care, poor medical care, lack of stimulation, and lack of motivation. As with learning disabilities, there is a broad range of possible causes and a broad range of manifestations, some easily detectable and some not.

Researchers at New Bedford Harbor estimate that 87 percent of those with developmental delays will be mildly affected and will be only a little slower than average in learning new information and skills. As children, their mental retardation is not readily apparent and may not be identified until they enter school (New Bedford Harbor, 1996). Many persons exhibiting developmental delays graduate from high school and work to support themselves. Some live independently in group homes, and others marry and have children of their own. There is a very wide range of abilities among those who are considered to be developmentally delayed. It is important to look at the whole person and to help all individuals to accomplish their greatest potential rather than focusing on limitations.

Have you ever tried to complete a task or participate in an activity and found it beyond your grasp (such as playing a sport you were not familiar with, trying to play a musical instrument, or beginning a class in a hard subject)? This is a very awkward feeling. List five feelings that you have experienced when placed in uncomfortable situations due to your lack of ability:

_____

_____

_____

Unfortunately, most people with developmental delays often experience the feelings you just listed. Now you can relate to the feelings of people with intellectual abilities different from the majority.

TERMINOLOGY    Here are some definitions relating to intellect that you should be familiar with:

**Developmental delay.** This refers to a limitation in one's ability to learn or care for him or herself. Once institutionalized for their condition, persons with developmental delays are now guaranteed the right to learn and grow to the best of their abilities.

**Down syndrome.** A genetically linked disorder caused by a chromosomal abnormality, Down syndrome is a common cause of developmental delays.

**Giftedness.** Characteristics of gifted students include outstanding performance on an achievement or aptitude test in one area such as mathematics or language arts, openness to experience, setting personal standards for evaluation, ability to play with ideas, willingness to take risks, preference for complexity, tolerance for ambiguity, positive self-image, ability to adapt readily to new situations, and ability to become submerged in a task (Gifted Resources, 1996).

**Gifted underachiever.** This is a general term for a talented student who does not achieve academic success. Gifted underachievers may not be interested in conforming to school rules, may be disinterested or bored with coursework, and may feel alienated from their classmates.

**Intelligence.** This refers to a person's capacity for reasoning, understanding, acquiring knowledge, and other forms of mental activity.

**Phenylketonuria (PKU).** This is a hereditary abnormality of the metabolism which can cause developmental delays.

EMPOWERMENT
TIPS

Following are some empowerment tips for dealing effectively with students of varying intellectual abilities (adapted from Karge, 1996).

* *Avoid using slang terms that refer to intellectual ability.* For example, "For someone so smart you're sure acting stupid," or "I've lost my car keys again—I'm so retarded."

* *Be consistent and fair.* Do not adapt an assignment for a student who is gifted or developmentally delayed unless the student requests that.

* *Teach self-discipline, hard work, and patience.* These are valuable qualities for students of any intellectual ability.

* *Encourage creative problem solving.* Guide students toward new ways of looking at problems.

* *Provide a safe environment for exploration.* Encourage students to learn at their own pace and experiment in their own way.

CLASSROOM
STRATEGIES

The following concrete strategies may prove useful when you face an entire classroom of students with intellectual differences.

* Examine "the big picture" before narrowing in on a topic. For example, discuss the workings of the human body as a whole before studying individual cells. Then present information and instructions in small, sequential steps. Review each step frequently (University of Connecticut, 1996).

* Use concrete materials that are interesting, age-appropriate, and relevant (University of Connecticut, 1996).

- Encourage students to let their particular interests guide them through the exploration of a topic.

- Provide prompt and consistent feedback (University of Connecticut, 1996).

- Encourage students to learn via computers. Computers allow students to progress at their own pace.

- Remind students that everyone has a unique talent which no one else on earth possesses. Encourage them to discover and use that talent.

- Teach tasks or skills that students will use frequently, in such a way that they can apply the tasks or skills in settings outside of school (University of Connecticut, 1996).

CLASSROOM SIMULATION

Finally, let's return to the scenario that opened this chapter. Read the situation below and record your reactions. Answering the questions will prepare you to handle intellectual diversity in the classroom. There is no one "right" answer.

|  |  |
|---|---|
| Setting: | Your classroom |
| Time: | During lunch break |
| Persons involved: | Linda Wan, a student with a developmental delay |
| Background: | After two years in special education classes, Linda now attends regular classes. She is fun-loving, enthusiastic about learning, shows promise as an athlete, and is a talented artist. |
| Circumstances: | Linda comes in to return a borrowed book. |
| Simulation: | Linda has seemed to be quite depressed lately. You've observed that she has not smiled once in the last week. You say, "Linda, you've looked pretty down lately. What's the problem?" She answers, "I just wish they'd leave me alone. Why aren't I like everyone else? Why do all the kids call me *retard*?" |

1. What are your objectives?

_____

_____

_____

2. What will you say to Linda?

_____

_____

_____

3. How else can you help Linda?

_____

_____

_____

4. What will you say to Linda's classmates?

_____

_____

_____

5. How might you prevent such an occurrence from happening again?

_____

_____

_____

CONCLUSION    What would you consider "average intelligence" to mean?  Consider your answer carefully.

_____

_____

_____

Remember as you try to define "average intelligence" that according to

U.S. government studies approximately one in four Americans reads below a fourth grade level. Intelligence does not mean only education—consider life skills, talents, and mechanical aptitude as well. Persons who are intellectually superior or who have significant intellectual deficiencies are contributing members of society. They deserve our respect in the same way that others who are diverse do.

Labels often become self-fulfilling prophecies. Rosenthal and Jacobson (1968) demonstrated that to some extent, children's performance can improve if teachers, relatives, and friends are led to believe they have superior ability. For example, students labeled as gifted stereotypically excel at most tasks, while students labeled as developmentally delayed stereotypically perform poorly. Our students actually learn to perform and conform to what is expected of them. When it comes to intellect, teachers should think of all children as organic computers—waiting to be turned on, given a purpose, and allowed the freedom to operate on their own.

REFERENCES       Alessi, N. (Ed.). (1992). Children who are mentally retarded. In *Facts for families.* [On-line.] Available: http://www.aacap.org/factsFam/retarded.htm

Gifted Resources. (1996). A short summary of giftedness. In *Gifted resources homepage.* [On-line.] Available: http://www.eskimo.com/~user/zbrief.html

Karge, B. D. (1996). Intellectual differences. In S. E. Schwartz & B. D. Karge, *Human diversity: A guide for understanding* (2nd ed.) (pp. 188-189). New York: McGraw-Hill.

New Bedford Harbor. (1996). Introduction to mental retardation. In *New Bedford Harbor services.* [On-line]. Available: http://www.ici.net/cust_pages/nbhsi/mr-def.htm

Rosenthal, R. & Jaconson, L. (1968). *Pygmalion in the classroom.* New York: Holt, Rinehard & Winston.

University of Connecticut. (1996). Overview of mental retardation. In *Department of mental retardation homepage.* [On-line.] Available: http://www2.uconn.edu/ctstate/dmr/overview.html

# Health Differences in the Classroom

OBJECTIVES

By the end of this chapter you should be able to answer these questions:

❧ What is the difference between acute and chronic health impairments?
❧ What problems do health impairments pose to our schools?
❧ Where can a teacher look for help for a student attempting to cope with health difficulties?
❧ How can a teacher help parents of children with medical conditions to adapt to the classroom in the least disruptive way?

THE CLASSROOM IS A MICROCOSM

*To the best of your knowledge, no one in your class has any health problems. Today you are showing a movie to your students. While the movie is running, one of your students yells, "Hey, look!" Everyone turns around and sees that Susan Brady has fallen to the floor and is having convulsions. Some of the students find the seizure to be funny, and a few students seem upset and frightened. Susan is unconscious, convulsing, and breathing.*

INTRODUCTION

No fewer than 10 percent of children in the United States have some form of chronic health impairment (Cushner, McClelland, & Safford, 1996). At least a million of those children suffer from diseases severe enough to require hospitalization and to regularly interfere with normal activities. In addition to these diseases, there are traumas from such things as physical assaults, sports injuries, and accidents involving automobiles, bicycles, skateboards, and boats. Emergency rooms treat more than three million children a year (Krementz, 1989).

## One Day in the Lives of America's Children

Every single day in the United States,

| | |
|---|---|
| 7,742 | teens become sexually active |
| 623 | teens get syphilis, gonorrhea, or H.I.V. |
| 2,795 | teens get pregnant |
| 1,106 | teens have abortions |
| 372 | teens miscarry |
| 1,295 | teens give birth |
| 689 | babies are born to mothers who have had inadequate prenatal care |
| 719 | babies are born at low birthweight (less than 5 pounds, 8 ounces) |
| 129 | babies are born at very low birthweight (less than 3 pounds, 5 ounces) |
| 67 | babies die before one month of life |
| 105 | babies die before their first birthday |
| 27 | children die from poverty |

Derived from Children's Defense Fund, (1996).

Clearly these challenges to children's health have an impact upon our schools, and may pose problems for the classroom teacher. Remember, however, that the large majority of chronically ill or injured children survive to adulthood, and knowledge and understanding of their health issues can help us to offer sensitive and appropriate assistance to them and their classmates (Krementz, 1989).

PERSPECTIVE
ONE

Imagine you have a serious disease and have been told you have only six months left to live. What will you do? How will you spend your time? Will your life have more authenticity due to your consciousness that it is limited?

_____

_____

_____

Perhaps you have devoted most of your time to your career. Will you now spend your time at home with your family? Or is your work so compelling and so important that you will continue it to the end?

_____

_____

These questions can help you to clarify your own priorities and to better understand some of the issues facing students with health challenges.

It is unlikely that most of us would give up our hobbies if our time were limited to six months. If we love painting, we would paint. If we enjoy sailing, we would sail. All those things which enrich our lives and give meaning to them would probably take priority. So why is it that we require a catalyst such as a death sentence to force us to commit to doing what we find most rewarding and enjoyable? We don't have to wait. We can choose to embrace life now, and by doing so

> **VOICES OF EXPERIENCE**
>
> *"Nobody can be in good health if he does not have all the time fresh air, sunshine, and good water."*
> —*Sioux Chief Flying Hawk*

perhaps influence the children in our tutelage to do the same. Can you think of some ways in which you might better prioritize your life?

_____

_____

Now that you have dealt with the news of your limited life span, consider another scenario. A wonder substance has been discovered. It is being added to water supplies all over the world. After today, the average lifespan is six hundred years. That calendar in your mind suddenly is more than seven times as long as you had previously constructed it. Six hundred years sounds like all the time in the world, doesn't it?

Continue the exercise your started earlier. How does knowing that you will live six hundred years affect your life choices?

_____

_____

_____

Where will you invest your time and energy, knowing that you have so much more time than you'd imagined? Which endeavors seem relevant over this long term?

_____

_____

Does your stake in the world seem different? Is your interest in the environment increased?

_____

_____

Are there books that you now feel you have time to read? What are they?

_____

_____

What good deeds will you do for your neighbor now that the pressures of time have been lifted?

_____

_____

Will you do nothing, feeling that there's no hurry? Or will you soon adjust your mind so that six hundred years seems short?  Write your thoughts below:

_____

_____

When you receive information that one of your students is affected by a health impairment, what is your first reaction?  What kinds of adjustments do you expect that you and the class will need to make?

_____

_____

_____

_____

_____

_____

Children with health impairments usually do not appear to be any different from other children, and they can engage in most typical school activities.  During periods of good health there may be no disease symptoms at all.  Health impairments include limited strength, vitality, or alertness.  Such impairments are frequently not noticeable to the general public unless an acute episode occurs.  Do you know the difference between an "acute" impairment and a "chronic disorder"?

_____

_____

_____

_____

### Spotlight
#### on the Classroom

*"I was 10 years old when my mother was diagnosed with leukemia.  It was as if we were all diagnosed.  My brother's, my sister's, and my life were changed forever.  We had the disease, too, in a way, because we had to deal with all the symptoms.*

*"Mom was hit unusually suddenly, and she went from healthy to unable to walk or feed herself in a matter of weeks.  It took everybody pulling together to cope with the added responsibilities and medical expenses.  We cried and cursed a lot, but we all pitched in.*

*"We learned a lot from Mom's strength and also learned a lot about our own ability to do what was required.  I missed a lot of school that first year, but my teachers were very understanding and helped me to make up the work.  They also taught me and my classmates about the disease.*

*"We actually got stronger individually and as a family in spite of all the hurt and worry.  People don't appreciate their health until they lose it."*
—W.S., student

136

Acute impairments are time-limited, while chronic disorders are considered to be treatable but not curable.  Can you think of an example of each?

_____

_____

Such things as diabetes are chronic, while injuries suffered in a fall might be acute.

Impairments may occur as the result of conditions present at birth or may result from disease.  Breakthroughs in medical technology extend life but often necessitate lengthy and costly treatments and hospital stays, often resulting in psychological stresses for both the child and the family.  Where would you look for help for a student attempting to cope with such difficulties?

_____

_____

_____

Advocacy and support groups are available for almost all categories of health issues.  If students with health impairments or their parents ask for your advice or are in obvious distress, you might encourage them to look for a network of people interested in the same issue who can help them learn to cope with the associated challenges.  What are some other responses you can give?

_____

_____

_____

No two health challenges are the same, nor do they affect people in the same way.  Each disease has individual causes, symptoms, cures, and interventions.  It is critical to support those around us in a loving manner.  Treating the children the same as we treat others and communicating with them about their health problems are two key ways we can improve the lives of these children without offering any medical or psychological advice.

A serious health issue which all of society faces is Acquired Immune Deficiency Syndrome (AIDS). AIDS is a life-threatening disease for which there is as yet no cure, but it can be prevented. AIDS education has become the responsibility of not only parents, teachers, and medical personnel, but of every thinking individual.

Human Immunodeficiency Virus (HIV) has been linked to the onset of AIDS. Not everyone infected with HIV gets AIDS. When one is infected with HIV, his or her immune system attempts to fight the virus but is unable to destroy it.

The spread of AIDS can be stopped through awareness, compassion, commitment, and community support for safer sexual activities. It is critical that an HIV antibody test be performed if AIDS is suspected. The test determines the presence of HIV antibodies in the blood. If there are antibodies present, the person is infected with HIV.

If the diagnosis is HIV positive, early medical help is one way to remain healthy. It is vital for those who are HIV positive (or at risk for HIV) to strengthen their immune systems. What are some ways to boost the immunity?

_____

_____

A proper diet, regular exercise, stress-reducing programs (such as meditation or other relaxation techniques), abstinence from drugs and alcohol, regular massage therapy, and loving relationships have all been shown to dramatically boost immunity and general well-being. Medical research into the treatment and cure of AIDS is ongoing.

Should children who are HIV positive or who have AIDS be allowed to attend school? Why or why not?

_____

_____

Though some teachers, parents, and students question the safety of having children with AIDS or HIV in the classroom, it is important to remember that professionals state that AIDS is not spread through such activities as coughing, sneezing, breathing the same air, eating together, or touching. HIV is spread through blood-to-blood contact, sharing bodily fluids during sexual contact, and breast milk. Pregnant women may be able to pass HIV to their babies before or during birth.

Another major health concern which affects growing numbers of teenagers, as well as children of increasingly younger ages, is alcohol and drug abuse. An estimated 14 million Americans abuse alcohol or illicit drugs to the point of dependence each year. What are some consequences for our school population of the increasing use of drugs and alcohol?

---

---

Pregnant mothers who abuse drugs place themselves as well as their babies at risk for a variety of serious and sometimes life-threatening problems which affect the children into adulthood. Seizures, shortness of breath, lung damage, nasal membrane burns, respiratory paralysis (by overdose), cardiovascular problems, anorexia, and premature labor are all examples of potential problems.

> **VOICES OF EXPERIENCE**
>
> *"Healing is a matter of time, but it is sometimes also a matter of opportunity."*
> —Hippocrates, "Father of Medicine"

Aside from the increased risk of impaired physical and intellectual well-being and accidental injury of themselves and others, what are some negative effects of alcohol and drug abuse by students?

---

---

There is a high rate of absenteeism, as well as inability to focus and learn. Teachers may face the problem of dealing with acute health problems in the classroom, as well, since overdose can lead to seizures and other health emergencies.

Besides alcohol, what is a commonly used drug which can be legally purchased by adults and is widely available to children?

---

Snuff, chewing, or smoking tobacco products are popular sources of the drug nicotine. Although the number of American men who smoke is decreasing steadily, the percentage of female smokers has been rising, as has use by children and teens, according to recent studies. As a result, today more women die of lung cancer than breast cancer each year. The use of snuff or chewing tobacco has increased in the U.S., and tobacco smoking in other parts of the world remains prevalent.

What are some arguments for smoke free schools, including faculty lounges and recreation areas?

_____

_____

Recent cancer studies have proven the dangers of secondhand smoke, and most government and public establishments—such as restaurants, schools, hospitals, and airplanes—are now designating themselves "smoke-free zones" to prevent an unhealthy environment. All cancers caused by smoking could be prevented entirely. Nicotine is highly addictive, and people in the process of breaking the habit may exhibit irritability, anxiety, cravings, headaches, and lethargy. Symptoms of withdrawal may continue for 4-8 weeks and cravings may continue indefinitely.

PERSPECTIVE
FIVE

Now let's look briefly at some other major areas of health concerns you may encounter in the classroom.

**Asthma** is a chronic respiratory condition in which breathing becomes difficult due to blocked air passages. It affects almost 10 percent of children in the United States (Bachman, 1992). Episodes of asthma can be triggered by emotional factors, which may tighten the muscles around the bronchial tubes and cause swelling of the tissues. Many new drug treatments successfully control the symptoms of asthma.

What are some actions you may be called upon to take in aid of children with asthma?

_____

_____

Children may need to leave class in order to go to the nurse for regular of periodic medication, or may need to keep inhalers or oxygen with them in class. The classroom environment itself may need adjustment if there are allergens such as pets or plants which seriously affect the child (Bachman, 1992).

Asthma attacks vary from child to child, and individuals react to different triggers. What are some special problems for the teacher in determining when to take action?

140

Children, particularly younger ones, may not realize or know how to express the fact that they are experiencing restricted breathing. Teachers need to be aware and to recognize symptoms and triggers (Bachman, 1992).

**Diabetes** is a metabolic disorder characterized by the inability to properly process carbohydrates. In other words, it affects the means by which the body changes the food we eat into energy. Typically, the pancreas fails to secrete an adequate insulin supply, resulting in an abnormal concentration of blood sugar in the blood and urine. Symptoms include excessive thirst, frequent urination, weight loss, slow healing of cuts and bruises, pain in joints, and drowsiness. Long-term problems could include blindness, kidney failure, and heart attacks.

How might you be called upon to assist a child with diabetes in your classroom?

---

---

You may need to make an exception to any rules against eating in class, as the child may need to eat a piece of candy or a glucose tablet. Children with diabetes must never miss any meal and must be permitted to snack, even during tests. You may be asked to keep Gatorade® or a similar product on hand since it is readily absorbed. Because children with diabetes are slower to heal than normal, it is important that even minor accidents be reported to the school nurse for treatment (Elliott, 1990).

**Epilepsy** is a chronic central nervous system condition characterized by periodic seizures, convulsions of the muscles, and sometimes a loss of consciousness. A major epileptic seizure is often dramatic and frightening to those who have little experience. Typically, a seizure lasts only a few minutes and does not require expert care. Epilepsy can be controlled by medication. Do you know what to do if a child has a seizure?

---

---

The child should not be moved unless there is danger of an injury from banging his or her head against on object. Do not put an object in the child's mouth. Loosen any tight clothing. Turn the child on his or her side so that no mucus or blood is inhaled. If the seizure lasts longer than five minutes, call an ambulance (Reisner, 1988).

There are many other severe illnesses which may affect the children in your classroom. These may include such diseases as cancer, hepatitis, sickle-cell anemia, and severe allergies. Should you have children with these or any other health problems, it would be wise for you to conduct your own research into these conditions and discuss the specific cases with the school nurse. This will ensure that your interactions with these children are proper and helpful.

TERMINOLOGY    Knowledge of the following additional health impairments is vital for all classroom teachers.

**Hemophilia.** This is a disease characterized by the blood's failure to clot after injury as well as profuse bleeding from even minor injuries. It is hereditary, found primarily in males because females carry the hemophiliac gene, passing it to male children.

**Leukemia.** This is cancer of the blood-forming organs. It results in an increase of white blood cells and progressive deterioration of the body.

**Rheumatic Fever.** This is characterized by acute inflammation of the joints, fever, nosebleeds, rashes, and nervous disorders. It can cause heart damage by scaring tissue and valves. It often appears after a streptococcus infection.

**Sickle-cell anemia.** This is a blood condition in which the red cells assume a sickle shape and impair circulation by not properly carrying oxygen. No cure is available for this condition. Any activity that reduces oxygen in the blood (such as hiking to high altitudes) may bring about a crisis. The symptoms are low vitality, pain, shedding of blood cells, interference with cerebral nutrition, and chronic illness. The condition is genetic and largely limited to persons of African descent.

**Tuberculosis.** This is an infectious, chronic and communicable disease. It most often affects lungs, but also destroys tissues of body organs and bones. A positive tuberculin skin test reaction can diagnose the disease. Properly treated, patients are cured.

Use the following empowerment tips to help cultivate healthy interactions with students and parents.

● *Never judge by appearances.* Many seriously ill children look healthy.

● *Keep a current certification in first aid.* Be well-practiced in emergency techniques.

● *Know whom to contact at your school and how to reach that person.* Know the chain of command in case your contact person, such as the nurse or the principal, is unavailable. You should know exactly who is to do what in the event of a medical emergency.

● *Put yourself in the place of the parents, who may at times seem to be overly protective of the child and overly demanding of you.* Imagine how you would feel and behave if your own child were ill, and be patient with their fears and uncertainties.

● *If you know that there is a chronic or serious health concern, ask parents for a written summary of the child's medical history.* Read the summary carefully before scheduling a conference so that you can ask informed questions.

● *Caring, understanding, attention, and touch are some of nature's most potent medicines.* Give your time, support, and encouragement and you will ease the stresses of being ill.

● *Know the medications a child must take.* See that he or she has the opportunity to do so as prescribed, either in the classroom or the nurse's station or office, as your school policy dictates.

● *Be inclusive rather than exclusive.* Involve the health challenged child in all activities that you would normally, depending upon his or her interests and abilities.

● *Talk about coping with the health challenge.* Since many health conditions are controlled rather than cured, it is appropriate to talk about coping with the ongoing symptoms. Nurture and promote positive coping mechanisms.

● *Listen to the child's and the parents' concerns.* Sometimes simply listening and hearing their feelings can be helpful to all of you.

● *Learn about the health-related services available in your school system and in your community.* Be prepared to access them as needed.

* *Seek an understanding of how it feels to both the parent and child to face a health challenge.* With learning comes growth and healing.

* *Keep abreast of potential problems.* Ask the school nurse or health aide to alert you to any health problems among your students which may require special precautions.

* *Act deliberately and calmly at all times.* Your appropriate behavior will serve as a model to your students, and help to allay their anxiety.

CLASSROOM
STRATEGIES

The following classroom strategies will prove useful in dealing with health impairments on a daily basis (adapted from Cain, 1996).

* Parents and classmates of children with health challenges need to be informed and educated. An understandable concern of parents is that a child's illness is not contagious. Assure them that contagious diseases are public health issues, regulated by the state. It may prove helpful to have health brochures handy for parents and students.

* Involve the parents of children with medical conditions in helping them to adapt to your classroom in the least disruptive way. They have knowledge and experience to share, and everyone concerned will benefit from a team effort.

* Collect reading materials for the classroom which will help students to understand both causes and treatments of diseases and disabilities. They will profit from information on medicines, hospitalization, and the feelings and coping methods of children with health challenges as well.

* When a child needs special attention in class, or requires the assistance of a classroom aide, be sure that all parents and students understand that it is the child's illness, and not the child, that is receiving special attention.

* Present lessons to your classes about various health problems. Your school nurse and community agencies should be excellent resources for your lessons.

* Treat all students alike. Do not pay undue attention to children with health challenges because this can single them out as "teacher's pets," and cause social problems with their peers. It also adds to their feeling of being different or vulnerable physically.

* Depending on the age of your students, arrange a class visit to a nursing home which specializes in caring for patients with health

impairments. While there, be sure to have your students notice the level of care that is required for some patients. Encourage students to maintain a journal of thoughts or questions about the patients or their illnesses.

CLASSROOM
SIMULATION

Finally, let's return to the scenario that opened this chapter. Read the situation below and record your reactions. Answering the questions will prepare you to handle health differences in the classroom. There is no one "right" answer.

|  |  |
|---:|:---|
| Setting: | Your classroom |
| Time: | During mid-morning class |
| Persons involved: | Susan Brady and the rest of your students |
| Background: | To the best of your knowledge, no one in your class has any health problems. |
| Circumstances: | You are showing a movie to your students. |
| Simulation: | While the movie is running, one of your students yells, "Hey, look!" Everyone turns around and sees that Susan has fallen to the floor and is convulsing. Some of the students find the seizure to be funny, and a few students seem upset and frightened. Susan is unconscious, convulsing, and breathing. |

1. What will you do immediately?

_____

_____

_____

_____

2. What else will you do?  In what order?

_____

_____

_____

_____

3. Look in an up-to-date first aid manual.  What are the correct first aid procedures for seizures?

_____

_____

_____

4. If you find out that Susan's health problem was not new, will you take any action concerning the fact that you weren't informed?  If so, what?

_____

_____

_____

5. How will you handle questions from your students about the event?

_____

_____

_____

CONCLUSION In response to rising health care costs, current trends in healing are focusing more and more on prevention and holistic health, which treats the entire person and his or her lifestyle, not merely the disease itself.  Today, hospitals and doctors' offices are not the only places one can turn to for help.  Where else can a person now turn for healing?

_____

_____

People with health issues are finding guidance, support, and treatment from dieticians, massage therapists, chiropractors, acupuncturists, herbalists, psychiatrists, physical therapists, exercise and fitness counselors, families, and friends.

The health and safety of your pupils is a major responsibility.  Most unexpected events that involve teachers are fairly minor and

146

should be handled logically and easily.  Some events require extreme care and immediate response.  Your greatest challenge, however, may be to keep in mind that children who suffer chronic illness, disabilities, or acute medical problems have often experienced more difficult situations, endured more pain and discomfort, and made more significant adjustments in their young lives than many adults will ever be called upon to do.  Remember that they are still children, in spite of their sometimes mature aspects, and approach them as you would any student, with sensitivity and respect for the individuals that they are.

REFERENCES    Bachman, J. L. (1992). *Keys to dealing with childhood allergies.* Hauppauge, NY: Barrons.

Cain, N. (1996). *Healing the child: A mother's story.* New York: Rawson Associates.

Children's Defense Fund. (1996). *S.O.S. America!* Washington, D.C.: Children's Defense Fund.

Cushner, K., McClelland, A., & Safford, P. (1996). *Human Diversity in Education.* New York: McGraw-Hill.

Elliott, J. (1990). *If your child has diabetes.* New York: Perigee Books.

Krementz, J. (1989). *How it feels to fight for your life: The inspiring stories of fourteen children who are living with chronic illness.* New York: Fireside Books.

Reisner, H. (Ed.) (1988). *Children with epilepsy: A parents guide.* Rockville, MD: Woodbine House.

# Communication Diversity in the Classroom

**OBJECTIVES**   By the end of this chapter you should be able to answer these questions:

- What are four ways that students communicate in the classroom?
- What are six common communication disorders?
- What is the best way to communicate with a student who is not proficient in English?
- What is the best way to handle speech and language disorders in the classroom?

**THE CLASSROOM IS A MICROCOSM**

*Mika Yamauchi, a new student in your class from Japan, seems to be adjusting well to her new school and circumstances. On her first day, you were pleased to see some girls invite her to sit with them at their lunch table. After lunch, however, Mika meets with you, obviously in distress. "Everyone hates me," she says, barely holding back tears. You ask her to explain why she formed this opinion. She replies, "At lunch they said, 'You have such beautiful hair! I hate you!'"*

**INTRODUCTION**

Communication is a relationship—a human connection. The word *communicate* comes from a Latin word which means "to share." Communication is a means of transmitting information, ideas, or feelings from one person to another. The ability to communicate often means survival, as when we need to signal our need for help. Communication is clearly the central cohesive element of the classroom—indeed, it is the linchpin of learning.

Through communication we share our knowledge, ideas, dreams, and hopes. Name at least four ways we communicate:

_____

_____

_____

**NON-ENGLISH LANGUAGE SPEAKING AMERICANS**

| Language | in millions |
|---|---|
| Spanish | 17.339 |
| French | 1.702 |
| German | 1.547 |
| Italian | 1.308 |
| Chinese | 1.249 |
| Tagalog | .834 |
| Polish | .723 |
| Korean | .626 |
| Vietnamese | .507 |
| Portuguese | .429 |
| Japanese | .427 |
| Greek | .388 |
| Arabic | .355 |
| Hindi | .331 |
| Russian | .241 |
| Yiddish | .213 |
| Thai | .206 |
| Persian | .201 |
| French Creole | .187 |
| Armenian | .149 |
| Navaho | .148 |
| Hungarian | .147 |
| Hebrew | .144 |
| Dutch | .142 |

(derived from Johnson, 1995)

We communicate in many ways, including speech, gestures, drawings, written language, sign language, and facial expressions. Language is the primary means by which people communicate. Ironically, however, it is also the primary means by which people *fail* to communicate. Anyone who has traveled has no doubt encountered either an unfamiliar dialect or a totally foreign language. In different cultures, people communicate with different gestures as well. Let's first look at the diverse ways in which people exchange ideas, then examine methods to break down communication barriers in the classroom.

PERSPECTIVE
ONE

Our reliance on language is so fundamental that we often take it for granted. It is through language that we organize our social structures and learn how to coexist. The communication of messages plays a vital role in expressing and transmitting our culture. In fact, culture itself has been defined as "any system in which messages cultivate and regulate relationships" (Gerbner, 1990, p. 423). Whenever you speak and write your language, you also speak and write your culture. The cultural assumptions and understandings of many generations are embedded in your words.

> **VOICES OF EXPERIENCE**
>
> *"The mystery of language was revealed to me. I knew then that 'w-a-t-e-r' meant the wonderful cool something that was flowing over my hand. That living word awakened my soul, gave it light, set it free."*
> —*Helen Keller, author and educator*

A culture's myths, legends, and folk ballads are products of communication. Before our ancient ancestors invented writing, they preserved their history through the "oral tradition." They recited or sang their history over and over again, thereby passing it down to the next generation. Over time, the stories changed and kept only the most important and profound meanings—ideas about the beginnings of life, the nature of humanity, and the mysteries of death. These stories survive today as mythology, folklore, legends, allegories, fables, and parables.

A culture's visual arts are another important product of communication. The earliest records of human communication are the prehistoric drawings on cave walls in France and Spain, depicting human figures and animals. To this day, art continues to serve as an important visual means of sharing information and imagination, whether in the form of a painting in a museum or an illustration in a magazine advertisement. Written language, too, can reach artistic proportions in poetry and literature. Even the alphabet itself can be a means of artful expression, as seen in calligraphic handwriting.

There are yet other facets of cultural communication found in the performing arts. Dance, for example, is a system of body language that expresses meaning through movement, gestures, poses, and pantomime. In many parts of the world, such as India, Japan, and Thailand, complex systems of pantomime and dance are combined with symbolic hand gestures, facial expressions, and body movements to tell a story (Crystal, 1987). Some of these dances have survived for thousands of years and communicate traditions and ideas from the past to every new generation. Similarly, opera combines singing, costumes, movement, and other modes of communication. Some people enjoy going to the opera even if they don't understand the words of the songs because they can understand the story through the universal language of gestures, facial expressions, and vocal intonations.

PERSPECTIVE
TWO

Body language is a form of nonverbal communication. Through posture, facial expressions, eye contact, and hand gestures, we can express our feelings, emotions, and attitudes. Waving a forefinger back and forth can say "You are wrong." Holding someone's gaze for a number of moments can indicate "I know you" or "I am interested in you." Leaning forward during a conversation can mean "I am involved in what you are saying."

Some body language is universal. For example, certain facial expressions or gestures signify pain, fear, and joy in every culture. However, other expressions may have different meanings in different cultures. Nodding one's head up and down, for instance, means "yes" in the United States and Europe but may mean "no" in other cultures (Beier, 1990).

In some cultures, touching is a very important part of communication. Touching can involve a wide variety of activities: embracing, holding hands, kissing, linking arms, nudging, patting, shaking hands, and slapping, just to name a few. Tactile activities express basic social interactions such as gratitude, greeting, and leave taking. Can you think of other social interactions expressed through touching?

_____

_____

_____

Sexual interest, aggression, congratulations, and affection can also be expressed through touch.

151

Some societies are more tolerant of touching than others. Northern Europeans and Indians, for example, tend to avoid touching, while Arabs and Latin Americans tend to favor it. In a study of couples sitting together in cafés, it was found that Puerto Ricans touched each other 180 times an hour while Londoners never touched at all (Crystal, 1987). This does not mean that Puerto Ricans are more affectionate than Londoners, just that in British culture communication is less tactile.

There is a science of "visible speech" called *eurhythmy*, in which the body symbolically interprets the sounds of language. Each sound that a person can articulate is reflected by a body movement. The sound *a*, for example, means astonishment and wonder and is shown by raising the arms over one's head as if holding a giant ball. The sound *u* means something is chilling and is expressed by pressing the arms and legs together. Sound, movement, and meaning come together in this intricate system of body language.

PERSPECTIVE
THREE

There are between 4,000 and 5,000 languages spoken around the world. Mandarin predominates, with 930 million speakers. English comes in a distant second, with 463 million speakers, and Hindi follows with 400 million (Hoffman, 1993). David Crystal (1987) has explained that all languages are "equal in the sense that there is nothing intrinsically limiting, demeaning, or handicapping about any of them" (p. 6). No one language is necessarily easier or more difficult to learn or speak than another—even the languages of primitive societies have complex grammatical rules.

> **VOICES OF EXPERIENCE**
>
> *"Communication is the back and forth of telling and listening and responding, so you know you are not alone."*
> —A. Brandenberg, author

Because every language meets the social and psychological needs of its speakers, the study of languages can provide our students with valuable insights into human nature and society (Crystal 1987). That's because a society's intellectual heritage and cultural traditions are directly shaped by the society's language. Name three benefits of being fluent in another language that you could cite to your students:

_____

_____

_____

If your students become fluent in another language, they will be able to read great books in the original language of the author and meet the great minds of another culture on their *own* terms. They will learn how other people think, and then they will truly understand another culture and appreciate its values. Ultimately, their own heritage will be enriched because they will see it from an outside perspective. If a student's native language is English, or if that student is in the process of learning English, he or she will discover that it has borrowed from many other languages.

There is as of yet no such thing as an international language. Through the Middle Ages, Latin was the language of education in western Europe. From the 17th to the 20th century, French was the international language of diplomacy. Today there are more Chinese speakers than any other, but the complexity of the Chinese writing system discourages its use. English has assumed special status internationally, though it is still not a world language. Attempts have been made over the years to design an artificial language—a new, simplified language that combines elements of natural languages—to serve as an international language. The artificial language Esperanto, invented in 1887 expressly as an international language, has millions of speakers worldwide and is sometimes used at international conferences. However, the United Nations has yet to grant Esperanto international status.

PERSPECTIVE FOUR

The age at which children develop language varies greatly. Generally speaking, however, we can safely say that the earliest communication begins with social interactions between the caregiver and the baby. For example, the caregiver may play peek-a-boo with the baby, point to and name objects, make facial expressions, and so on.

> ### *Spotlight*
> #### *on the Classroom*
>
> *"I've lived in the U.S. since I was five, and my sister was born here. I'm not a U.S. citizen, I'm Chinese, but I've grown up like an American and gone to school here all my life. The only Chinese people I know are my parents. They speak Chinese at home and live as much a traditional Chinese life as they can. It's an advantage to understand two languages and cultures, but it's hard, too, because culturally I'm an American.*
>
> *"My parents are often shocked and disturbed over things my friends' parents wouldn't even notice. For instance, a female classmate sent me a Christmas card last year. My mother saw that the girl had written "I hope all your hopes and dreams come true," and she got hysterical. She thought that meant that we were having sex.*
>
> *"My friends can't really understand my Chinese culture, either. They don't see how I can put my responsibility as the oldest son before everything else. To them, challenging their parents is part of growing up. To me, it's the opposite. I want to live like them, but the Chinese part of me is too strong to make it worth the guilt."*
> —Lee P., student

During the first half-dozen months, babies typically experiment with vocalizing simple sounds. This "cooing" gradually becomes a string of babbling, and at about age one the child may put different syllables together and may have learned to "answer" when spoken to.

Between ten and eighteen months, children usually say their first words. At this stage they often echo what they hear without understanding the word or mispronounce a word and therefore remain misunderstood. At about a year and a half, they typically make their first two-word combinations, such as "more juice."

At two years, children begin to effectively communicate with simple sentences and a vocabulary of several hundred words. After age two, the child's vocabulary and grasp of the language continues to grow. However, because the development of language varies so greatly from child to child, it is often difficult to properly diagnose communication disorders at an early age.

Several million people in the world are unable to communicate effectively with others because of speech or language problems. The National Institute of Health estimates that over fourteen million Americans alone experience such difficulties (Voice Foundation, 1994). The problem is magnified immeasurably because anyone who tries to communicate with a person with a speech or language disorder may also experience difficulties. Speech and language disorders inevitably draw attention to themselves, and the awareness itself may inhibit communication. The challenge, then, is to overcome this barrier, not to create yet a further problem with communication. With information and understanding, we can avoid this pitfall.

Speech and language disorders are actually quite different. An individual with a speech disability usually has some level of difficulty in communicating because of such characteristics as an incorrect pronunciation of words or parts of words, or a lack of fluency when saying words or phrases.

While the person with a speech disorder may have problems expressing him or herself, the person with a language disability may have either an expressive or a receptive difficulty. When an individual has an expressive language problem, that person is able to correctly produce the sounds necessary for speech but the words themselves may be used incorrectly or illogically. A person who has a receptive disorder has no known hearing difficulties and usually has knowledge of the meaning of words. However, the individual may have difficulty comprehending what has been correctly heard.

Students with communication disorders may face a variety of troubling issues. Can you think of three possible issues that may arise?

_____

_____

_____

Typical issues include ridicule from others, classroom problems, finding support, finding role models and mentors, relationships, labeling, finding the "right" type of treatment, finding acceptance, and others considering them either less or more intelligent. Later on, these students may have trouble finding a job that accepts or is willing to recognize communication challenges.

If any of your students has a speech or language disorder, the best way to help is to be informed about support services in your school and community. Local chapters of service organizations, such as the American Speech-Language-Hearing Association, may be able to provide information on communication disorders and educational programs. Speech and language therapists in your school or in private practice and in hospitals may be able to provide information on scientific research and methods of treatment. Speech and language therapists and local organizations also may be able to refer your student to a support group which meets regularly.

TERMINOLOGY The following list of terms presents an overview of common communication disorders. Your familiarity with these disorders will help prepare you to deal with them and teach about them in the classroom.

**Aphasia.** This condition is usually caused by brain damage and is characterized by labored speech and an inability to choose the right words.

**Articulation problems.** A difficulty with pronunciation or a lisp is an articulation problem. People with articulation problems may experience anxiety and embarrassment, which interferes with communication.

**Cleft lip and palate.** A cleft lip is a congenital splitting of the upper lip. A cleft palate is a congenital fissure along the middle of the palate. Both conditions may affect the development of speech, but not in all cases. Surgery is usually very successful in treating this problem.

**Dyslexia.** This is an inability to read and spell correctly, despite normal intelligence. Frequently, letters become reversed or out of order.

**Fluency disorders (stuttering).** This disorder of fluency affects one's ability to control the rhythm and timing of speech. Stuttering often involves a repetition of sounds, syllables, words, or phrases. Though people who stutter may speak with difficulty, this has nothing to do with their intelligence. People who stutter frequently experience anxiety and embarrassment, and communication is invariably affected.

**Illiteracy.** The inability to read and write is called *illiteracy*. One in five Americans is functionally illiterate, meaning they do not have the reading or writing skills required to function effectively in society. Often illiteracy is the result of another disorder such as vision impairment, hearing impairment, or dyslexia.

**Laryngeal abnormalities.** Malignant growths in the throat may require surgical removal of the larynx. Persons who have undergone an laryngectomy must learn to speak by vibrating their esophagus or by using an artificial larynx which, when placed against the neck while they are talking, emits a speech substitute which is often characterized as having a "buzzing" sound.

**Muteness.** This is the inability to speak, due either to a physical abnormality or to emotional stress (as when someone "loses her voice").

**Vocal problems.** Raspy, hoarse, nasal, breathy, weak, or abnormally loud voices may make someone difficult to understand. Disorders of vocal expression are usually due to an anatomical abnormality in the vocal tract, such as the formation of nodules or polyps.

EMPOWERMENT TIPS

Below you will find empowerment tips for various types of communication styles and disorders. Teach these techniques to your students and model them yourself.

❧ *Language differences.* It is sometimes necessary to be patient and understanding when speaking with someone from another country. It may help your patience to imagine yourself speaking someone else's native tongue. It is difficult to hear and speak a foreign language, and people from other countries are not always proficient in English. They may not be used to making the foreign sounds of our language. Mistakes in pronunciation or grammar do not mean that they are uneducated or unintelligent. Such mistakes just mean that they are in the process of learning another language. If you speak slowly and clearly, it will help others to understand you. However, raising the volume of your voice will not accomplish anything.

🖋 *Illiteracy.* Offer help without making any judgement about the person's inability to read and write. Give clear, simple directions or draw a map showing landmarks. As with other disabilities, do not assume illiteracy means low intelligence. Be sensitive to feelings of embarrassment.

🖋 *Fluency and articulation disorders.* Try not to allow a stutter or a lisp to dominate your attention. You may end up missing what the person is saying and embarrassing him or her at the same time. Just as with a nonnative speaker, remember that hesitant speech does not indicate slowness of thought. Be patient and relaxed, and listen carefully rather than attempting to speak for the other person.

🖋 *Eye contact.* Different cultures have different customs about eye contact. Some societies favor prolonged eye contact, while others find prolonged eye contact to be rude or threatening. If you notice that someone from another culture is either averting her eyes or holding them on yours for too long, keep in mind that she may be following different rules of etiquette. Generally, it is best to try to find a middle ground if you are unsure. Body language expert Julius Fast recommends that you break eye contact frequently as you talk or listen. Look down to the side and then back (Fast, 1994).

🖋 *Hand gestures.* As with eye contact, hand gestures are closely linked to culture. Some people use few hand gestures (such as the Japanese) and may seem stiff or standoffish to one who uses sweeping, expressive gestures (such as the Italians). Again, different rules of behavior may apply. Before making generalizations about any individual, try observing for a while.

🖋 *Personal space.* We may feel uncomfortable when strangers invade our "body space." However, how one measures the comfort zone depends upon one's culture. The normal·social interaction distance can vary significantly among peoples. Be aware if the person is instinctively inching closer to you or farther away, and try to accommodate his comfort zone. As with eye contact, when you are unsure, try a middle ground.

CLASSROOM STRATEGIES

Use the following classroom strategies to create a safe environment which fosters open and easy communication.

🖋 Keep foreign language dictionaries in the classroom. Occasionally pull one out during a conversation, saying, for example, "Hmmm... Let's see what the Italian word for *photosynthesis* is."

🖋 Make eye contact, give a smile, nod your head, and say hello to every one of your students during the course of your day.  Encourage your students to do the same with their classmates.

* Learn three phrases in another language (from a book in the library or from a friend) and teach them to your students.

* Learn how to say "I would like to communicate with you" in sign language.  Teach your students how to sign this sentence.

* Distribute index cards and instruct your students to draw a picture expressing how they feel that day.  Have them show their card to anyone who asks "How are you doing?"

* Teach your students that the following stereotypes of people with communication disorders are *not* true:

  • People with communication disorders tend also to have a low IQ.
  • Stuttering is an indication of an extremely high IQ.
  • Articulation disorders are easy to correct.
  • A person with a cleft palate always has difficulty speaking.
  • People with communication disorders have emotional disorders as well.
  • A language disorder by definition means difficulty with speech.

* Have your students imagine that they are not literate or are encountering an unknown language.  Ask how they would feel when confronted with the following message on a bottle: ΠθχλδλΣ: Ωζδϖζλ! Ψζ λζβ Ψχδλη!

* Suggest to your class that they observe the body language of the people around them at lunch today.  Can they tell if someone is intrigued, or bored, or excited by a conversation?  Do they touch each other, and if so, where and how often?  Characterize their proximity to one another and thereby determine how well acquainted they are.  Have your students share their findings after lunch.

Finally, let's return to the scenario that opened this chapter. Read the situation below and record your reactions. Answering the questions will prepare you to handle communication differences in the classroom. There is no one "right" answer.

Setting: Your classroom

Time: Just after lunch

Persons involved: Mika Yamauchi, a new student in your class from Japan

Background: This is Mika's first day in your classroom. She seems to be adjusting well to her new school and circumstances.

Circumstances: You were pleased to see some girls invite Mika to sit with them at their lunch table today.

Simulation: After lunch, Mika meets with you, obviously in distress. "Everyone hates me," she says, barely holding back tears. You press her to explain why she formed this opinion. She replies, "At lunch they said, 'You have such beautiful hair! I hate you!"

1. What are your objectives?

_____

_____

_____

2. How do you explain to Mika what happened?

_____

_____

_____

3. How do you explain to Mika what the girls really meant?

_____

_____

_____

4. What do you say to your class about communication differences?

_____

_____

_____

CONCLUSION

We take our language and our customs for granted, and it's easy for young people to unconsciously feel that theirs is the "only way." But such an attitude is a hinderance to good communication among people of different languages and cultures. Communication allows young people to share in the experience of being alive. It gives them the opportunity to grow and to evolve individually and collectively.

Your students' ability to communicate effectively may break down when they meet someone who has a physical impairment which creates a difficulty in speech or language, or when they are ignorant about the ways they can choose to send and receive information. Teach your students that they cannot fail to be richer when they connect with a fellow human being. If they make this effort, they will always be rewarded.

REFERENCES

Beier, E. (1990). Body language. *Encyclopedia Americana* (International edition, vol. 4, pp. 131-32). Danbury, CT: Grolier.

Crystal, D. (1987). *The Cambridge encyclopedia of language.* Cambridge: Cambridge University Press.

Fast, J. (1994). *Body language in the workplace.* New York: Penguin Books.

Gerbner, G. (1990). Communication. *Encyclopedia Americana* (International edition, vol. 7, pp. 423-24). Danbury, CT: Grolier.

Hoffman, M. (1993). *The world almanac and book of facts 1994.* Mahwah, NJ: Funk and Wagnalls.

Johnson, O. (Ed.) (1995). *1996 information please almanac.* Boston: Houghton Mifflin.

Voice Foundation. (1995). *The voice foundation.* Philadelphia: The Voice Foundation.

# Behavior Differences in the Classroom

**12**

OBJECTIVES

By the end of this chapter you should be able to answer these questions:

❧ What are some factors which influence a child's responses and behaviors?
❧ What do we mean by temperament?
❧ How can you more effectively deal with behavior and personality differences in the classroom?
❧ What are the identifying signs of hyperactivity?
❧ What are some warning signs of suicide?

THE CLASSROOM IS A MICROCOSM

*You are administering a test during the last period of the day. Jennifer, one of your students, begins tapping her pen on her desk in a rhythmic pattern, distracting the other students from their work, as evidenced by their looking up to locate the source of the noise. You look at Jennifer, raising your eyebrows meaningfully, and she meets your eye. As soon as you return to your work, the tapping resumes.*

INTRODUCTION

Among the categories of human diversity, children with behavior and personality disorders are perhaps the most misunderstood. Despite progress in many areas, the education, treatment, and integration of such persons into communities remain subject to debate among parents, community members, legislators, and educators. There is no denying that a small percentage of people who have behavior and personality disorders act in ways that are extremely offensive, even to the most tolerant among us. It is important to keep in mind, however, that this is true of a very small percentage of the population, and frequent interaction with such individuals is not likely. In this chapter, we will explore some behavior and personality differences among children which may affect their academic and social success. As a teacher, you will need to be familiar with personality and behavior differences so that you can identify problems and respond to them appropriately.

6-10% of the population exhibits problems relating to behavior and personality.

We know that every child has his or her own personality traits and learning style. What are some factors which influence all of us in our reactions and responses, just as they influence our students?

_____

_____

_____

Such factors as birth order, age, gender, disabilities or health problems, family crises, sibling competitions, family values, socioeconomic status, and cultural and ethnic differences all affect behavior and social interaction. It is important not to overlook these differences when we consider the appropriateness of behavior in the classroom.

Sometimes children grow up with good role models. Their parents, guardians, and other significant adults work hard at teaching acceptable behavior, but still the children behave in ways which are considered inappropriate as they grow up. Many of your students, unfortunately, may not have the benefit of adults in their lives who guide their behavior and serve as good role models. Some young people may come from homes where one or both parents are abusive, where older siblings are disruptive, and where socially unacceptable behaviors are the norm. Children who exhibit disruptive behavior in school may be imitating the only model they have had.

What are some examples of behavior differences you might expect to encounter in the classroom which would be disruptive enough to require action on your part?

_____

_____

_____

Such disruptions as repeated outbursts from a student, cursing, interfering with another student's work, or physically or verbally attacking someone are some examples. Others might be the failure of a student to interact at all, but to be noticeably withdrawn, to sleep in class, or to show signs of an eating disorder. A student might appear constantly nervous or anxious, or be fearful of speaking out in class. Some behaviors are situational or temporary, but consistently unusual or inappropriate behavior needs help.

Can you think of some examples of situations which might trigger a temporary behavior problem in class?

_____

_____

_____

_____

The death or illness of a family member or friend, a divorce or other life change such as a move or the birth of a sibling, or even a physical change such as new braces or glasses may affect a student so that there is a noticeable change in behavior temporarily.

PERSPECTIVE
TWO

We will explore in depth some causes of behavioral differences later in this chapter. For now, suffice it to say that most patterns of behavior develop during an individual's formative years. The following disturbing statistics may help to illustrate some influences on today's young people. Every day in the United States over 1200 teenagers give birth, at least five teenagers commit suicide, over 1800 children are physically, emotionally, or sexually abused, over 3000 children run away from home, over 1500 children will spend the night in a jail which was designed for incarcerated adults, and approximately 3000 children will learn that their parents are going to be divorced (Eaton and Schwartz, 1996).

> **VOICES OF EXPERIENCE**
>
> *"From the moment of his birth the customs into which [an individual] is born shape his experience and behavior. By the time he can talk, he is the little creature of his culture."*
> —*Ruth Fulton Benedict, anthropologist*

What psychological consequences do you suppose these young people may suffer?

_____

_____

_____

You can see that problems like school failure, dropping out, drug and alcohol abuse, chronic physical and emotional problems, and, ultimately, suicide, may be the result of behavior and personality problems which have their roots in early childhood.

As teachers, we are uniquely situated to observe these problems and to address them so that there is hope for positive change. It is vitally important, however, to keep in mind that we are not psychologists, physicians, or judges. What then, is the teacher's role in the life of a student who shows signs of a behavior or personality problem?

_____

_____

_____

Our observations are valuable, and we can play a crucial part in changing social behavior and in giving children a new sense of themselves by the way we interact with them. However, it is not our role to treat illnesses, mental or physical, nor to diagnose any child. In cases where treatment is needed, our role is to refer the student for appropriate help to a physician or mental health professional.

PERSPECTIVE
THREE

In order to distinguish between normal behavior differences and significant problems, we first need an understanding of how human beings all differ. Every individual has a natural, inborn style of behavior, which we can call his or her temperament. This is not associated with motivation, but rather is a description of *how* an individual behaves in a certain circumstance. We can influence temperament by our interactions and by control of the environment, but we cannot change or cause temperamental characteristics (Turecki & Tonner, 1985).

> **Spotlight**
> **on the Classroom**
>
> *"Many of a child's behaviors are predictable if you know his style profile. And, forewarned, you can more easily plan an effective learning program to reduce liabilities and increase assets."*
> —Simon and Bryam, educators

Dr. Stanley Turecki (1985), a noted child psychiatrist, has described nine traits which we can use to identify and describe the way a child interacts with his environment:

1) Activity level. How active is the child generally?

2) Distractibility. Can the child pay attention? How easily is he or she distracted?

3) Persistence.  Can the child stay with something he or she likes?

4) Adaptability.  How does the child deal with change, or with transition from task to task?

5) Approach/withdrawal.  How does the child initially react to newness?

6) Intensity.  How loud is the child usually, whether happy or unhappy?

7) Regularity.  How predictable is the child in physical habits?

8) Sensory threshold.  How does the child react to noise, lights, smells, or temperature?

9) Mood.  Is the child predominately negative or positive?

(Turecki & Tonner, p.14)

Clearly, students with lower activity levels, less distractibility, more adaptability, less intensity, and more positive moods are easier to deal with in the classroom.  However, those with the opposite, "difficult" attributes are not necessarily abnormal, according to Dr. Turecki.  "Abnormality," he explains, "implies the presence of a clear diagnosable disorder.  Human beings are all different, and a great variety of characteristics and behaviors falls well into the range of normality" (Turecki & Tonner, 1985, pp. 15-16).

PERSPECTIVE
FOUR

Most students who have diagnosed behavior or personality differences will have been assessed for placement in special education, or have prescribed medications, or both.  What so-called "difficult" children would you expect to encounter most often in the classroom?

_____

_____

_____

The best known developmental disorder of the eighties and nineties is Attention Deficit Disorder, or Attention Deficit Hyperactivity Disorder (ADHD).  This disorder can affect a child's school performance, self-esteem, and ability to behave in appropriate ways in a social or academic setting.  Some researchers believe that ADHD is simply a normal human variation, the way that height, intelligence, or athletic ability are.  Accordingly, in a typical classroom there will be students who can concentrate all day long, and some who are extremely easily distracted from their tasks (Garber, Garber, & Spizman, 1995).

ADHD differs from a learning disorder in that ADHD is usually diagnosed on the basis of the individual's ability to cope with everyday life rather than by a standardized test. It is characterized by inattention, impulsivity, and hyperactivity (Weaver, 1995). Typical behaviors of a person with ADHD include fidgeting, blurting out answers, difficulty waiting for his or her turn, talking excessively, being easily distracted from a task, interrupting, and difficulty sitting quietly.

What is the teacher's role in regard to students with ADHD?

_____

_____

_____

_____

The teacher's role is to help each student find the optimal way of learning, while establishing and maintaining an orderly classroom environment. The teacher should be ready to refer any students whose needs are clearly not being met for expert evaluation and help.

What environment is best for the student with ADHD? What are some strategies for teaching him or her?

_____

_____

_____

_____

According to Dr. Stephen Garber (1995), problems of the child with ADHD may be exacerbated by school if he or she is required to participate in the wrong kind of experience. Garber says that more structured settings are best for the child with ADHD, and that classroom routines and consistent consequences, both negative and positive, are best. Whenever possible, distractions in the classroom should be minimized, and academic tasks broken into smaller parts (Garber, Garber, & Spizman, 1995).

When a child often seems overly worried in a nonspecific way, or is in constant need of reassurance, there is a possibility that he or she is experiencing anxiety. Anxiety affects the child's ability to succeed in school because he or she cannot concentrate. It inhibits his or her ability to enter into new experiences, and it negatively affects self-esteem (Doft, 1992).

Can you think of some ways of helping children who experience anxiety in the classroom?

_____

_____

_____

Creating situations where the child can succeed and gradually grow in confidence may help. Small steps in mastery can lead to a willingness to try new things. However, if you observe that the child's anxiety does not lessen, or that it interferes with his or her academic or social life, you should request a professional evaluation (Doft, 1992).

Another common disorder is depression. Depression does not affect only adults. Even the youngest children may suffer from depression. Can you name some symptoms of depression in childhood?

_____

_____

_____

The child who is listless, seems uncharacteristically sad, has trouble concentrating, or is acting out in ways that are not typical of him or her, may have depression. Sometimes depression is also masked as anger, and attention should be paid to the child who is exhibiting any of these symptoms. If you notice persistent symptoms which you cannot identify as situational, (for example, a family crisis) then you should take them seriously, and seek help for child (Doft, 1992).

Depression is sometimes associated with suicide. Even the youngest child may talk of suicide, or engage in very risky, dangerous behavior such as jumping off a building. You should know some warning signs which may signal distress so severe that it could lead to suicide. Here are some of the most common warning signs (adapted from Kolehmainen & Handwerk, 1986, p.15-17):

1) The person has previously attempted suicide.

2) The person talks about death or suicide.

3) There is a noticeable change in the personality or mood of the individual, for which there is no obvious explanation.

4) There are changes in sleep and eating patterns, which may be noticeable at school.

5) The person in distress may withdraw from friends and his or her usual activities.

6) The person who is suicidal may take unusual risks, such as driving recklessly, which show a disregard for life.

7) There may be uncharacteristic drug or alcohol abuse, or abuse of prescription drugs.

8) The person may make final arrangements, write farewell letters, or give away possessions, or attempt to conclude unfinished business.

What can you do to help a student in despair?

_____

_____

_____

_____

If you have observed some of the above warning signs in a student, one of the best approaches is to ask questions. Kolemainen & Handwerk (1986) explain that questions allow you to get information you need to make an assessment of the situation and show your interest at the same time. Ask the student such questions as why he or she is so unhappy, whether anyone else knows about this unhappiness, what would make things better, and what you can do to help right now. Ask questions and listen rather than trying to offer answers and solutions. Involve other professionals by referring the student to a counselor immediately, and follow up to be sure someone is helping (Kolemainen & Handwerk, 1986). You also should discuss serious situations with your principal to ensure that all necessary resources are made available to be sure that school district policies are followed.

When children break rules of the classroom or act inappropriately, whether because of a personality or behavior difference or because of a particular situation, the teacher must respond. That response may result in a consequence or in a punishment. Curwin & Mendler (1990) have explained that consequences teach responsibility, while punishments teach obedience through fear. Punishments include measures such as spanking, threats, lectures, loss of privileges, scolding, or humiliation. Punishments are not directly related to the rule which has been violated. Consequences follow naturally and logically from the child's actions. They are directly related to the rule which has been broken, and that connection is obvious to the child (Curwin & Mendler, 1990). The following chart illustrates the difference:

| Punishment | Consequence |
| --- | --- |
| Attacks dignity of the child | Enhances dignity of the child |
| Is externally oriented | Is internally oriented |
| Focuses on the past | Focuses on the future |
| Gives short-term results | Gives long-term results |
| Is not related to the rule | Is related to the rule |

(Adapted from Curwin & Mendler, 1990, pp.56-57)

Name some examples of a punishment:

_____

_____

_____

Such things as standing a child in the hall or in a corner, berating, isolating, and threatening the loss of privileges are punishments.

What are some examples of consequences?

_____

_____

_____

Consequences teach the child a lesson he or she can internalize, without a loss of self-esteem. For example, a forgotten homework assignment might mean redoing it during what is usually free time. That consequence would encourage the child to be more responsible, without labeling his or her behavior negatively.

Curwin & Mendler (1990) have suggested the use of three kinds of consequences: predicting, choosing, and planning. *Predicting* is simply asking the child what will happen in the future if he or she repeats the inappropriate behavior. *Choosing* is giving the child a choice from several alternative behaviors. *Planning* is asking the child for a solution to the problem (Curwin & Mendler, 1990, p.57-59). Why do you think predicting, choosing, and planning would be effective means of encouraging appropriate behavior?

_____

_____

_____

_____

_____

This approach is effective because it involves the child in the solution to the problem. Of course, it is necessary to tailor this response to the child's age and ability to understand.

What are some situations where consequence-oriented responses might not accomplish your goal?

_____

_____

_____

Sometimes children must immediately obey, with no explanation at all. For example, when safety is involved, such as during a fire, a sudden emergency, or an assault upon one child by another, there may be no time for discussion.

TERMINOLOGY Following are some common terms relating to behavior and personality differences that you may encounter and should be familiar with:

**Anxiety.** Children who are anxious may fear interaction with others, react negatively to new situations, or exhibit irrational fears.

**Attention Deficit Hyperactivity Disorder.** This is the inability to focus on a task for a sustained period of time, along with the tendency to act impulsively. Individuals with attention deficit disorder may also exhibit hyperactivity.

**Autism.** This is an incapacitating disability affecting nonverbal and verbal communication and two-way social interaction. It affects one out of every 2,500 children. Typical characteristics include repetitive movements, abnormal responses to sensory stimulation, avoidance of eye contact, and insistence that routines remain unchanged.

**Bipolar Depression.** This is characterized by high-to-low mood swings, impulsivity, and high distractibility.

**Depression.** Persons may be depressed if they display a sad mood, have a persistently sad facial expression, and demonstrate many of the following symptoms nearly every day for a minimum of two weeks : poor appetite, sleep changes, motor restlessness, lack of activity, loss of usual interests, signs of apathy (Rosenberg,1995).

**Disruptive.** A child who is disruptive may start fights, demonstrate self-abusive behavior, try to draw attention to himself or herself by making noises, or generally generate a loss of order in the environment.

**Manic Depressive Disorder.** Manic depressive symptoms include episodes of extreme sadness, hopelessness, chronic fatigue, and irritability.

**Mood swings.** This refers to patterns of significant change in values, attitudes, compliance, friends, attire, and/or priorities.

**Phobic disorders.** A person with a phobic disorder has an unreasonable, recurring fear of a specific object, activity, or situation. Most people have some phobias, such as fear of heights, certain animals, flying, or public speaking. When a fear drastically interferes with everyday life, a phobia is present.

**Schizophrenia.** This should not be confused with multiple personality disorders. Schizophrenia involves a disturbance in thinking patterns that causes a person to act and speak strangely. People with schizophrenia may experience hallucinations and delusions.

**Temperament.** This refers to character traits with which we are born. Sometimes we refer to temperament as disposition. It is the basis of our personality.

**Tourette's Syndrome.** This is an inherited, neurological disorder involving involuntary, rapid, nonrhythmic motor movements or vocalizations.

EMPOWERMENT
TIPS

Take advantage of the following empowerment tips to improve your interactions with students who behave differently.

- *Keep your sense of humor.* Humor reduces stress and tension (Curwin & Mendler, 1990).

- *Examine your attitudes about control and discipline.* Do you believe learning must be work? Do you believe that discipline dampens a child's creativity? Do you believe that children respect only what they fear? Do you think you must be tolerant of rude or disruptive behavior? (Kvols-Riedler, 1979).

- *Avoid power struggles.* Turn as much responsibility as possible over to the student (Curwin & Mendler, 1990).

- *Establish and maintain a relationship of equality and mutual respect* (Kvols-Riedler, 1979). Such a relationship will create a safe environment for all students.

- *Establish clear, specific rules.* Stick to these, but limit them to the necessary minimum (Curwin & Mendler, 1990).

- *Have more than one perspective.* Know when it's appropriate to bend the rules (Weaver, 1995).

- *Give positive reinforcement at every opportunity* (Curwin & Mendler, 1990). Never miss an opportunity to reward good behavior.

The following classroom strategies may prove useful in educating about and dealing with behavior and personality differences in the classroom.

● No one is perfect.  If your attempts sometimes fail, you may find this checklist useful, adapted from Bill and Kathy Kvols-Riedler (1979, p. 244), experts on redirecting children's misbehavior:

____ I made sure that I did not make a child suffer.

____ My tone of voice was not condescending.

____ The child felt liked and accepted by me.

____ I encouraged the child to voice his or her opinion.

____ I respected the child.

____ I recognized the purpose for the misbehavior.

____ The child did not feel overpowered by me.

____ I avoided talking too much.

____ The consequence was logical.

____ I presented an alternate way for the child to feel special.

● Disruptive behavior is often an expression of frustration.  Honor learning differences as well as personality and behavior differences by involving students in projects that allow many alternative modes of expression, such as art, language, and music.  Engage them in writing essays in math, for example, or doing cartoons in English.  This brings a greater diversity of symbol systems into the subject matter, and allows every student the chance to find a means of expression of his understanding (Perkins, 1992, p.67).

● Ask yourself how the child sees the situation.  Consider possible causes of his or her behavior (Kvols-Riedler, 1979).

● Look directly at the child when correcting inappropriate behavior.  Don't speak to him or her from across the room, but make personal contact by getting close and at eye level (Kvols-Riedler, 1979).

● Respond with action and limit your verbal responses (Curwin & Mendler, 1990).  This will help you avoid turning disruptive situations into a battle of wits.

● Gain insight into the child's mistaken goal. Then help the child identify his or her mistaken goal in a nonaccusing way. Watch the child's facial expressions and body language to gauge whether your corrections are discouraging or frightening, rather than informing (Kvols-Riedler, 1979).

● Provide opportunities for the child to be helpful, to cooperate, to participate, and to do what he or she can to make the situation more enjoyable (Kvols-Riedler, 1979). This strategy will yield a wide spectrum of positive results.

● Learn more about ADHD and the various problems it can solve. Understand that ADHD indicates nothing about a student's intelligence (Weaver, 1995).

● The best way to handle all types of behavioral diversity in the classroom is to take a course in behavior management techniques. These techniques will allow you effectively manage the students without disrupting the learning process.

CLASSROOM SIMULATION

Finally, let's look again at the opening scenario. Read the situation below and record your reactions. The process of answering the questions will help you prepare for handling behavior and personality differences in the classroom. There is no one "right" answer, so be thoughtful and be yourself.

Setting: Your classroom
Time: The final class period of the day
Persons involved: Jennifer, one of your students
Background: Jennifer often exhibits some behavior problems.
Circumstances: Your students are taking a test.
Simulation: Jennifer begins tapping her pen on her desk in a rhythmic pattern, distracting the other students from their work. You look at Jennifer, raising your eyebrows meaningfully, and she meets your eye. As soon as you look away, the tapping resumes.

1. What are your objectives?

_____

_____

_____

176

2. What does Jennifer seem to want?

_____

_____

_____

3. How do you handle the situation?

_____

_____

_____

CONCLUSION

As Dr. Richard Curwin and Dr. Allen Mendler (1990) have written, it is of utmost importance for teachers to learn ways of addressing children's different learning styles. Concentrating on disabilities and weaknesses may worsen a student's poor self-esteem and contribute to greater disciplinary problems and academic failure. Attaching negative labels to those who are different and attempting to remediate them into being like everyone else can be extremely damaging, according to Curwin & Mendler. It is important to give positive messages about what children can do rather than what they cannot do. Our focus must be on their strengths, not their weaknesses (Curwin & Mendler, 1990).

REFERENCES
Curwin, R. L. & Mendler, A. N. (1990). *Am I in trouble? Using discipline to teach young children responsibility.* Santa Cruz: Network Publications.

Doft, N. (1992). *When your child needs help: A parent's guide to therapy for children.* New York: Crown Trade Paperbacks.

Eaton, L, & Schwartz, S. (1996). *Exceptional people study guide.* Gainesville, FL: Department of Independent Study by Correspondence.

Garber, S. W., Garber, M. D., & Spizman, R. F. (1995). *Is your child hyperactive? Inattentive? Impulsive? Distractible?* New York: Villard Books.

Kolehmainen, J. & Handwerk, S. (1986). *Teen suicide.* Minneapolis: Lerner Publications Company.

Kvols-Riedler, B. (1979). *Redirecting children's misbehavior: A guide for cooperation between children and adults.* Gainesville, FL: National Parenting Instructor Network.

Perkins, D. (1992). *Smart schools: From training memories to educating minds.* New York: The Free Press.

Rosenberg, B. A. (1995). *Depression in children.* Philadelphia: Cornerstone Psychiatry Associates.

Turecki, S. & Tonner, L. (1985). *The difficult child.* New York: Bantam Books.

Weaver, C. (1995). *Success at last! Helping students with attention deficit (hyperactivity) disorders achieve their potential.* Portsmouth, NH: Heinemann.

# Sensory Diversity in the Classroom 13

OBJECTIVES

By the end of this chapter you should be able to answer these questions:

- ❧ What factors can disrupt the hearing process?
- ❧ How exactly is hearing loss classified?
- ❧ What distinguishes "deaf" from "hard of hearing"?
- ❧ What are three causes of visual impairment?
- ❧ How exactly is a visual impairment classified?
- ❧ What is the definition of legal blindness?
- ❧ How can the classroom teacher best handle sensory differences?

THE CLASSROOM IS A MICROCOSM

*Shubha Rajsekaran's hearing aid has gone off again. A high-pitched whine fills the classroom. Shubha's level of hearing loss makes her oblivious to the sound, and she is confused by the sudden twittering of her classmates. "Somebody needs to check her batteries," mutters Tonya, sitting behind Shubha. When another student gives Tonya a frown, Tonya replies, "Don't worry, 'Deaf-and-dumb' can't hear me anyway!"*

INTRODUCTION

We use our senses—hearing, sight, smell, touch, and taste—to gather the information which we require to function safely and effectively in the world. Author and lecturer Helen Keller rejoiced in sensory experience. She wrote at length about life's abundant aromas, tastes, touches, and feelings. The fact that she could neither see nor hear did not diminish her zest for the sensory world. She was able to enjoy music by placing her hands on a radio, to read literature in Braille, to communicate with her friends through sign language, and to write down her wisdom and experiences.

As Helen Keller demonstrated by expressing her ideas and emotions, people with hearing or vision impairments do not think differently than other people. Nor do they necessarily lead impoverished lives. The purpose of this chapter is to examine the broad range of hearing and vision impairments and suggest methods for fuller, more enjoyable, and more effective communication with those individuals.

Hearing and vision facilitate learning, assimilate culture, and aid communication.

Hearing is the sense we use primarily in the development of language and speech. Since speech is the means by which we communicate with others, it is a fundamental factor in all social interactions. Hearing facilitates learning, and through hearing and speech we pass on our cultural values and our heritage. Vision, too, is important for assimilating our culture. We read printed words in books, watch the moving images in films, and study the intricate details in paintings. As with any culture, deaf and blind cultures celebrate their ancestors, heroes, victims, survivors, and trailblazers.

The culture of deafness is quite rich. From the ancient Greek historian Herodotus to the French novelist Guy de Maupassant, people have written eloquently about their own deafness or the deafness of friends and loved ones (Ackerman, 1990). Brian Grant's anthology *The Quiet Ear* compiles writings about deafness that span many different eras and cultures, and the play *Children of a Lesser God*, by Mark Medoff, has been made into a powerful movie. The German composer Ludwig van Beethoven, who became totally deaf at age 46, wrote his greatest music during his later years.

Just as with deafness, blindness has not hindered the productivity of some of our great cultural figures. The Argentine poet and story writer Jorge Luis Borges, many of whose works have been translated into English, was blind. Joseph Pulitzer, the prominent journalist, publisher, and congressman, went blind at the age of 40 but continued his various activities during the remaining 24 years of his life. James Thurber, the well-known magazine writer, dramatist, and cartoonist, lost the sight of one eye in a boyhood accident and the sight of the other as an adult. And the Greek poet Homer, author of the famous epics *The Iliad* and *The Odyssey*, was blind.

Let's explore the senses of hearing and vision in a little more depth, each in turn.

PERSPECTIVE ONE

*Hearing.* What exactly does *hearing* mean? To a porpoise, hearing is a kind of sonar, like a bat's, that brings back three-dimensional images more like sights than sounds. A porpoise can "hear" all sorts of details about a shark—its size, texture, motion, direction, and distance. If you go to a rock concert, you may *feel* the pulsing rhythm vibrating in your chest cavity. What hearing entails often depends upon the hearer and the context. Our range of hearing also depends upon which tools we use to extend it. What tools do you use to augment your hearing?

A stethoscope allows us to hear someone's heart beating. Loudspeakers make it possible to hear an orator in a large auditorium. With a telephone we can hear someone in another part of the world. A radio telescope allows us to hear the distant echoes of outer space. And a hearing aid amplifies the volume of the sounds around us.

Of all the senses, hearing offers perhaps the greatest potential for information because of its flexibility. While taste, touch, vision, and to a lesser extent smell require our proximity to the source, hearing potentially offers information about objects and events when all other senses are useless. Can you name a situation which might demonstrate this potential?

_____

_____

_____

We may hear a siren in the dark outside from our bedroom, for example, and be able to tell that there is an emergency or a fire nearby. We may be able to judge the distance and direction, and even determine if the siren is from a fire truck or police car, fairly accurately by using our sense of hearing.

Nobody can escape the world of sound. As sensory expert Diane Ackerman observed, even if we don't hear the outside world, we hear the throbbings and buzzings and whooshings of our own bodies. Many who are legally deaf can hear gunfire, low-flying airplanes, jackhammers, motorcycles, thunder, and other loud noises. Hearing disabilities don't protect us from ear distress, either, since we use our ears for more than just hearing. What else do we use our ears for?

_____

_____

Our ears help us keep balance and equilibrium and tell the brain how our head moves (Ackerman, 1990).

PERSPECTIVE
TWO

Our ability to hear is the result of a complex sequence of events. The outer ear collects sound waves and channels them through the auditory canal. The eardrum conducts sound waves through three tiny bones in the middle ear. The third bone is connected to the inner ear, which houses the cochlea. Here highly specialized cells translate vibrations into nerve impulses that are sent directly to the brain.

181

Our range of hearing can be affected by a variety of circumstances. Factors present before, during, or after birth can disrupt the hearing process. Childhood ear infections, loud concerts, gunshots, fireworks, and loud noises at work all have the potential to reduce one's hearing acuity. Even the natural process of aging gradually reduces our ability to hear high frequencies. According to researchers at Idaho State University (1996), ninety percent of young children's knowledge is attributed to incidental reception of conversations around them. Thus, learning is hindered even with the slightest hearing loss. Hearing is the basis of classroom learning—children spend at least 45% of the school day engaged in listening activities (Idaho State University, 1996).

There is no single phenomenon of "deafness," but rather a wide spectrum of hearing loss, from mild impairment to total deafness. We use the term *hearing impaired* to refer to all individuals who have a hearing impairment, regardless of its severity. A hearing loss is reported in decibels (dB) and is generally categorized as:

- mild (27-40 dB)
- moderate (41-55 dB)
- moderately severe (56-70 dB)
- severe (71-90 dB)
- profound (91+ dB)

A person with mild hearing loss may experience difficulty with faint or distant speech. A moderate loss makes speech beyond five feet difficult to understand. A person with severe loss is unlikely to hear a loud voice if it is more than one or two feet away, though he or she may be able to distinguish between different environmental sounds. Finally, a person with profound loss may be able to hear only very loud environmental sounds.

It is estimated that eight million children throughout North America have some degree of

> ### Spotlight
> #### on the Classroom
>
> "My child, Juanita, was born with normal hearing. Today, she cannot hear a single word, but she lives an independent and fulfilled life. At age seven she developed spinal meningitis, which resulted in a severe hearing loss in both ears. Her teachers, mother, and I all worked closely with her to retain the speech that she had acquired prior to the loss.
>
> "Juanita spent the first half of her elementary school years in a special program for children with hearing impairments. Then she entered a regular classroom. As an adolescent, she graduated with honors from the neighborhood high school. She decided to continue her education at the university level, earning an undergraduate degree in international relations and then completing law school.
>
> "Now Juanita is an attorney. She actively volunteers for local charities and spends her leisure time doing photography, collecting stamps, and rollerblading."
> —R.M., parent

hearing loss. That represents one in every six elementary students (Idaho State University, 1996). Approximately 80% of lower elementary students (4-10 years old) suffer from a temporary hearing loss sometime during the school year, often caused by an inflammation in the middle ear. The average hearing loss of these students is 25-30 dB, which is equivalent to plugging the ears with fingers (Idaho State University, 1996).

PERSPECTIVE
THREE

People with hearing impairments communicate through speech, lip or speech reading, or sign language. Depending upon the severity of hearing loss, one may use hearing aids to amplify sounds or have an electronic cochlear implant which aids the individual by stimulating nerve endings when sound is perceived. Obviously, hearing loss increases the challenges a person faces in daily living, but it does not necessarily prevent one from succeeding in the classroom, enjoying life, or attaining his or her goals.

Telecommunication devices (TDDs), resembling small typewriters, can be hooked up to telephones to allow people who are hearing impaired to carry on a telephone conversation. Captioned films and closed-captioned television offer subtitled dialogue. Signaling devices, using vibrations or flickering lights, can alert people with hearing impairments when the doorbell rings, the alarm clock goes off, or the baby cries. Telephone companies also offer "Relay Services" which allow an individual with a hearing impairment to engage in communication with a hearing individual in a manner equivalent to those individuals who are able to use standard voice telephone services. Relay Services utilize employees who use TDDs the same way an interpreter would.

Sign language classes are frequently included in community education programs offered by high schools, community colleges, and universities. Police and fire departments often train in basic sign language to be better prepared to communicate in any situation. Sign language interpreter services are typically offered in places of worship and at public events. Interpreters are also on-call 24 hours a day in many communities to assist in emergencies such as accidents and arrests.

TERMINOLOGY

Following are some common terms relating to hearing loss that you should be familiar with:

**Bilateral loss.** This is a hearing impairment in both ears.

**Conductive loss.** This is a hearing impairment that is located in the outer or middle ear. With proper amplification, sounds will be heard without distortion.

**Deaf.** This is a hearing loss so severe that it generally is not helped by amplification. Someone with total deafness must rely upon vision as the primary means for developing communication.

**Hard of hearing.** This refers to a hearing loss that does not prohibit the development of speech and language skills, with or without amplification.

**Postlingual hearing loss.** A hearing impairment that occurs after speech and language skills have been acquired is called "postlingual." A student with postlingual loss may have no difficulty with speech and language.

**Prelingual hearing impairment.** A hearing impairment that occurs either at birth or before speech and language skills have been acquired is called "prelingual." A student with prelingual loss may have difficulty mastering language and speech.

**Sensorineural loss.** This hearing impairment is located in the inner ear or along the auditory nerve to the brain. Even with amplification, sensitivity to sounds is reduced and/or distorted.

**Tinnitus.** This refers to a range of noises in the ear (typically a ringing or hissing) that can disrupt hearing.

**Unilateral loss.** This is a hearing impairment in only one ear.

EMPOWERMENT
TIPS

Take advantage of the following empowerment tips to improve your communication with individuals who have impaired hearing.

- *Learn sign language.* If you are skilled in some basic signs, you'll be able to communicate more comfortably and fully.

- *Speak in moderate tones.* Raising your voice or exaggerating your speech may only distort your facial expressions and make you more difficult to understand.

- *If you are not understood, rephrase rather than repeat what you said.* Rephrasing your thoughts may make your point more clear, and the person will have a second chance to understand you.

- *During group discussions, speak one at a time.* Too many people talking at once can be confusing to anyone, with a hearing impairment or not.

⚫ *If you are communicating through an interpreter, speak directly to the person with the hearing impairment.* Keep in mind with whom you are talking. The interpreter is just there to interpret.

CLASSROOM STRATEGIES The following classroom strategies may prove useful in educating about and dealing with hearing impairments in the classroom.

⚫ *Keep the classroom as quiet as possible.* The maximum desirable noise level for children having normal hearing is 35 dB, yet with 25 students and one teacher, the noise level can reach 60 dB, which is nearly twice the level appropriate for most children to clearly hear the teacher (Idaho State University, 1996).

⚫ *Teach some basic signs to your students.* Enable your students to demonstrate to persons with hearing loss that they wish to communicate.

⚫ *A light touch on the arm is appropriate to get the attention of a student with a hearing impairment.* To avoid possible offense, do not touch other parts of the body and do not wave your hand in an exaggerated fashion.

⚫ *Make sure the student with a hearing impairment can see your face clearly.* Avoid turning away, moving around excessively, or obstructing your mouth.

⚫ *Teach your students that the following stereotypes of people with hearing impairments are* not *true:*

  • All people with hearing impairments can read lips.
  • Sign language is a very limited form of communication.
  • People with hearing impairments are not as challenged as those with visual impairments.
  • The inability to hear is a sure sign of aging and/or senility.

⚫ *Teach your students that it is impossible to make generalizations about people with hearing disabilities.* Few people have perfect hearing. People with hearing impairments experience the same feelings and emotions as everyone else. They also have the same potential for fulfilling their dreams and living dynamic, interesting lives.

⚫ *Assign this homework:* Watch an entire prime-time television program, either comedy or drama, with the sound off. Discuss in class: Were you able to follow the show? What things proved helpful to your understanding? What things contributed to your confusion?

Vision. In the absence of light, everyone is blind. Photons of light bounce randomly off the objects around us, but it is the millions of rods and cones in the human retina that capture the light and send it through the optic nerve to the brain. Then the brain translates the photons into meaningful vision. Through the visual process, we observe the world around us and assimilate knowledge. In what ways do you rely upon your eyes?

_____

_____

We rely upon our eyes to direct us through our environment, to inform us through the written word, and to give us pleasure. But eyesight isn't the only means by which we can perceive the world.

What do you see when you walk into a room? An old friend? A boring co-worker? A beautiful landscape painting? An expensive vase? Much of what we "see" is wholly subjective. Our eyes do not technically "see" an old friend, but rather the figure of a person. We "see" the relationship in our minds. Whether the painting is beautiful or not, and whether the co-worker is boring or not, are also opinions we form in our minds (Chopra, 1991). What we see with our eyes is certainly important, but visual information is clearly only one part of observation. A person with no eyesight might touch your face and "recognize" that you are her friend or think that you resemble someone else. Blindness and visual impairment affect *how* information is obtained, but not necessarily *what* information is obtained.

Though blindness conjures up images of total darkness in the minds of the general public, only a small number of people are totally blind. Even people who have been totally blind since birth are greatly affected by light, Ackerman noted, because light influences us in many subtle ways. "It affects our moods, it rallies our hormones, it triggers our circadian rhythms [biological cycles recurring at 24-hour intervals]" (1990, p. 249).

We extend our field of vision in all sorts of ways. What are some tools you use to augment your vision?

_____

_____

Many people use eye glasses, contact lenses, magnifying glasses, telescopes, cameras, binoculars, microscopes, X-rays, and magnetic resonance imagers, just to name a few.

Some people must augment their vision due to a physical problem with their eyes. At least twenty percent of the population has some visual problems (Reynolds and Birch, 1982), but most of these cases can be corrected to the extent that the problem is not serious. It is estimated that approximately 1,440,000 individuals of all ages have visual impairments that are significant enough to limit their activities (LaPlante, 1991). The figure of one-tenth of one percent of the population is frequently cited for the prevalence of those people who are legally blind.

The term *visually impaired* describes a wide range of people with partial or complete loss of sight. Visual impairment may be either present at birth or acquired later through injury to the eye or brain. Visual disability may be due to:

> **VOICES OF EXPERIENCE**
>
> *"The responsibility for tolerance lies in those who have the wider vision."*
> —*George Eliot, author*

- refractive problems (farsightedness, nearsightedness, blurred vision, cataracts)
- muscle disorders (uncontrolled rapid eye movements, crossed eyes)
- receptive problems (damage to the retina and optic nerve).

Visual impairment is classified into three general categories: profound, severe, and moderate. With profound visual disability, one's performance of the most basic visual tasks may be very difficult. With severe visual disability, extra time and energy are needed to perform visual tasks. With moderate visual disability, visual tasks may be performed with the use of special aids and lighting.

PERSPECTIVE FIVE

People with visual disabilities use various types of adapted equipment to assist them at work, school, and throughout daily life. Some are quite ordinary, such as black felt tip markers that produce darker print, adjustable lamps to increase the amount of light and adjust its direction, large-type books, bifocals, contact lenses, magnifiers, tape recorders, friends, and guide dogs. More sophisticated technological aids include computers with speech output and enhanced screen images, Braille printers, and optical scanners and readers.

The local Division of Blind Services offers a wide range of information, from how to receive mobility training, how to obtain a guide dog, and where to find Braille newspapers or reader services. Public Radio, in many communities, also provides reader services by reading new books and the daily newspaper each day.

The fact that a person has a visual impairment tells us nothing about what he or she is like, what he or she can do, or even how much he or she can see. Blindness is not debilitating. The general public's attitudes and prejudices are more likely to be a handicap than the visual disability itself.

TERMINOLOGY · Following are some common terms relating to vision loss that you should be familiar with:

**Amblyopia (lazy eye).** This common condition involves poor vision in an eye that did not develop normal sight during early childhood. Amblyopia affects 2 or 3 out of every 100 people (American Academy of Opthalmology, 1995).

**Blindness.** A person who is totally without the sense of vision or has only light perception is considered to be blind. Such a person must learn primarily through touch and hearing.

**Farsightedness.** This refers to a condition in which one can see objects at a distance more clearly than those near at hand.

**Legal blindness.** Visual acuity of 20/200 or worse in the best eye with correction is considered to be legal blindness. This means that an individual can read at 20 feet what a person with normal vision can read at 200 feet.

**Nearsightedness.** This refers to a condition in which one can see distinctly at a short distance only.

**Tunnel vision.** This describes a field of vision limited at its widest angle to 20 degrees or less. A normal field of vision is generally measured on a horizontal arc of 160 to 180 degrees. A person with severe tunnel vision is considered to be blind.

**Partially sighted.** People who are partially sighted have a visual acuity greater than 20/200 but less than 20/70 in the best eye after correction. People who are partially sighted are able to use their vision as a primary source of learning.

**Low vision.** People with low vision have limitations in distance vision but are able to see objects and materials within a few inches or feet.

**Residual vision.** Any usable remaining vision is called "residual vision." For example, if an individual can detect only light, he or she can use that ability to an advantage.

Take advantage of the following empowerment tips to improve your interactions with people who have impaired vision.

- *Use a normal tone and volume of voice.* People with visual impairments do not necessarily have trouble hearing, so speak naturally.

- *Speak first and identify yourself.* Always let the person know who you are before he or she has to ask.

- *Use the person's first name.* Using the person's first name will make it clear who is being addressed.

- *Be precise when describing something.* Provide a reference point, such as "next to the door you came in" or "to your immediate left, about shoulder level."

- *Indicate the end of a conversation.* This will avoid the embarrassment of leaving a person speaking when no one is actually there (American Foundation for the Blind, 1995).

- *Don't assume that help is needed.* Ask if you can help, and then follow the lead of the person.

- *Guide persons who request assistance by allowing them to take your bent arm just above the elbow.* Walk ahead of the person you are guiding. Never grab people by the arm and push them forward (American Foundation for the Blind, 1995).

- *Give tactile clues.* Be aware that the person may rely on other senses to provide information. You can help to provide tactile clues: "Joan, let me take your hand and show you the skirt I just made."

- *Feel free to use words that refer to vision during the course of conversations.* Vision-oriented words such as *look, see,* and *beautiful* are perfectly acceptable (American Foundation for the Blind, 1995).

- *Feel free to use visually descriptive language.* Making reference to colors, patterns, designs, and shapes is perfectly acceptable (American Foundation for the Blind, 1995).

The following classroom strategies may prove useful in educating about and dealing with visual impairments in the classroom.

● *Teach your students that it is impossible to make generalizations about people with visual disabilities.* Few people have perfect vision. People with visual impairments experience the same feelings and emotions as everyone else. They also have the same potential for fulfilling their dreams and living dynamic, interesting lives.

● *Teach your students that the following stereotypes of people with visual impairments are* not *true*:

  • All people who are blind have superior musical talents.
  • People with visual impairments automatically develop heightened senses of smell, touch, hearing, and taste.
  • People with visual impairments are able to detect obstacles with a "sixth sense."
  • People who are legally blind have no functional vision at all.
  • People with visual impairments cannot go out without assistance.

● *Assign this homework:* Blindfold yourself upon getting out of bed in the morning, then do everything you normally do to get ready for the day, including taking a shower and getting dressed. (Be careful!) Discuss in class: What three things did you find difficult, frustrating, or even frightening? What three things were you able to do which surprised you?

Finally, let's return to the scenario that opened this chapter. Read the situation below and record your reactions. Answering the questions will prepare you to handle sensory differences in the classroom. There is no one "right" answer.

| | |
|---:|:---|
| Setting: | Your classroom |
| Time: | Early morning |
| Persons involved: | Shubha Rajsekaran, a student with a hearing impairment |
| Background: | Shubha's hearing aid sometimes emits a high-pitched sound. |
| Circumstances: | A high-pitched sound fills the classroom. Shubha's level of hearing loss makes her oblivious to the sound, and she is confused by the sudden twittering of her classmates. |
| Simulation: | "Somebody needs to check her batteries," mutters Tonya, a student sitting behind Shubha. When another student gives Tonya a frown, Tonya replies, "Don't worry, 'Deaf-and-dumb' can't hear me anyway!" |

1. What are your objectives?

_____

_____

_____

2. What do you say to Shubha?

_____

_____

_____

3. What do you say to Tonya?

_____

_____

_____

4. What do you say to your class as a whole?

_____

_____

_____

5. How might you prevent such situations in the future?

_____

_____

_____

CONCLUSION    It is impossible to make generalizations about people with hearing or visual disabilities. Few people have perfect hearing or perfect vision. Students with sensory impairments experience the same feelings and emotions as everyone else. They also have the same potential for fulfilling their dreams and living dynamic, interesting lives.

Ackerman, D. (1990). *A natural history of the senses.* New York: Random House.

American Academy of Opthalmology. (1995). What is amblyopia? In *Amblyopia FAQS.* [On-line.] Available: http://www.eyenet.org/public/faqs/amblyopia_faq.html

American Foundation for the Blind. (1995). Sensitivity to blindness or visual impairments? In *Information center.* [On-line.] Available: gopher://gopher.igc.apc.org.5005/00/info/general/sensitiv

Chopra, D. (1991). *Unconditional life.* New York: Bantam Books.

Idaho State University. (1996). Facts about children at educational risk with hearing problems. In *Department of Speech Pathology and Audiology Home Page.* [On-line.] Available: http://www.isu.edu/departments/spchpath/trai/facts.htm

LaPlante, M. P. (1991). The demographics of disability. In J. West (Ed.), *The Americans with Disabilities Act: From policy to practice* (pp. 55–80). New York: Milbank Memorial Fund.

Reynolds, M. C. & Birch, J. W. (1982). *Teaching exceptional children in all America's schools.* Reston, VA: Council for Exceptional Children.

# Notes

# Family Issues in the Classroom

OBJECTIVES    By the end of this chapter you should be able to answer these questions:

ᴥ What are three ways a family prepares its children for social interaction?

ᴥ What are some implications for the classroom teacher when a child is experiencing the divorce of his or her parents?

ᴥ Why must teachers concern themselves with child abuse?

ᴥ What is the process family members may go through when accepting a member who stands out as being "different"?

ᴥ What is the most current definition of *family*?

THE CLASSROOM IS A MICROCOSM

*The Kaplans, parents of your student Anna, are pleasant people whom you have come to know quite well, or so you thought. During a regularly scheduled parent conference, Mr. Kaplan briefly discusses Anna's good performance in your class. Then he tells you that they have a very serious problem and would appreciate your advice. When you agree to listen, they indicate that they have decided to get a divorce. Their concern is with whom Anna should live. They each want Anna, and they asked Anna with whom she wants to live. She told her parents she would go with the one you recommend. They then ask for your recommendation.*

INTRODUCTION

The vital functions that families provide for their members are complex. They aren't things that one can summarize into a tidy list and post on the refrigerator door. Intricate and subtle connections, interactions, involvements, and interrelations take place which help all the members to develop and thrive. Just as it is important for parents to support their children, it is equally important for parents to receive assistance, encouragement, admiration, respect, and affection from nearby

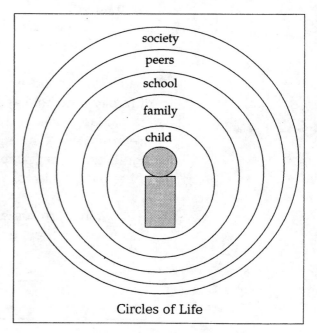

Circles of Life

relatives, friends, neighbors, fellow employees, and teachers. The quality of an individual's life is equally tied to family dynamics and to social interactions beyond the family.

Nancy Seufert-Barr, writing for the *United Nations Chronicle*, noted that "the family is a universal phenomenon—throughout the centuries and throughout the world" (Seufert-Barr, 1994, p. 1). Families are manifested in a wide variety of forms, however, and the idea of the family's role varies greatly among cultures. There is no such thing as a "typical" American family. Families fit no standard size, socioeconomic level, country of origin, age, religion, race, or makeup by gender or sexual orientation. However it is defined, the family unit is responsible for providing basic necessities of life, including shelter, comfort, food, security, friendship, love, attention, and a sense of worth and dignity.

The most important learning environment for any child is the family. Why might this be so?

_____

_____

_____

_____

It is within the family that children learn what it is to be a person. It is there that they learn the emotional, behavioral, and value patterns which form their identities and set up their social interaction with the rest of the world (Dwinell & Baetz, 1993).

What children learn is dependent upon factors such as what type of family they belong to, their racial heritage, ethnicity, socioeconomic status, language, and level of education, and the family's ability to prepare them to be a part of the larger culture. All these factors have a significant impact upon a child's success in school, and the importance of breaking cycles of school failure is clear.

What are some ways in which the educational level of the parent may have an effect upon the child?

_____

_____

Studies have shown that "children growing up with uneducated parents who are not poor are more likely to live in damaging conditions than are children who grow up with educated, poor parents. Children who grow up with an uneducated parent also have more school troubles than do children who grow up with poor parents. They are more likely to be in the bottom half of the class and to be retained a grade than are children who are poor only" (Weissbourd, 1996, p. 25).

PERSPECTIVE
ONE

Family structure in the past was largely based on one of two types, nuclear and extended (Seufert-Barr, 1994). How would you define a nuclear family? An extended family?

_____

_____

_____

_____

Nuclear families usually are made up of just two generations, parents and their children. These include single parent and adoptive families. Extended families include several generations and may be built upon a social rather than a biological basis. Nontraditional families are becoming more and more common. Can you think of some examples of nontraditional families?

_____

_____

By nontraditional we mean families based on cohabitation, same-gender, single parent, and reorganized, or step families (Seufert-Barr, 1994).

Historically, most families have been patriarchal, but with the industrial revolution came profound changes in the structure of the family. Urbanization caused different work and life styles which contributed to the dissolution of extended families, as well (Seufert-Barr, 1994). Until fairly recently, the traditional nuclear family was made up of a father, a mother, and children living together in the same home. The father was the primary wage-earner, and the mother stayed at home to care for the children. What percentage of families do you think fit the model of the traditional nuclear family today?

_____

Nuclear families make up less than 10 percent of American families today (Cushner, McClelland, & Safford, 1996).

Our definition of family continues to change as society changes. What are some new definitions of family that have become standard with societal changes?

_____

_____

New definitions include adoptive, foster, and migrant families as well. Families may be made up of stepparents and siblings, relatives, single parents, or a parent and a partner. Children may be raised by grandparents, aunts, uncles, siblings, neighbors, or friends. We define families as the primary source of the child's care, support, and sense of belonging, whatever the demographic makeup of the household.

What particular problems would you think migrant families might experience?

_____

_____

Migrant families may be adjusting to a new culture and language or dialect as well as to frequent moves. They may be living at a low socioeconomic level as well, and could be without the health or social welfare resources others might have.

According to Weissbourd (1996), as many as half the children in the United States born in the first part of the 1990s will be children of divorce. What are some implications for the classroom teacher when a child is experiencing the divorce of his or her parents?

_____

_____

Children may act out, test their teachers to see whether they will be abandoned, or deliberately cause trouble in the hope that it will draw their parents back together. They may be withdrawn or depressed, or too absorbed with personal matters to concentrate in class (Weissbourd, 1996).

While ideally the family is a refuge and source of strength, comfort, and protection for its members, far too often children suffer from abuse, violence, and neglect within the home.  Can you define child abuse?

_____

_____

_____

Child abuse can be defined as behavior which negatively affects a child's physical or emotional health.  Sexual abuse ranges from nonphysical to violent.

In what strata of society would you expect to find abusive family members?

_____

Abuse takes place in families of every category of wealth, education, race, geographic location, and ethnicity.  No one is necessarily immune.

Why must teachers concern themselves with child abuse?

_____

_____

_____

The problems of abuse affect every classroom in the United States.  Even if no child in a particular classroom is a victim of abuse, the climate is pervasive, and it colors our worldview.  We cannot ignore the reality of the family crises so many of our students experience, because these children bring the effects of abuse to the classroom and teachers may be called upon to respond in a variety of ways.

Aside from the physical consequences of abuse, what are some effects which might show themselves in the classroom?

_____

_____

_____

A child who has been abused may suffer from depression. He or she may be unable to focus, and may be too preoccupied by problems at home to concentrate on academic work (Greenberg, 1994).

How widespread is the problem of abuse? What percentage of students would you assume to have had some experience of sexual or physical abuse?

_____

Social researchers now believe that one in three or four girls will be sexually abused by age eighteen. One in eight to ten boys will be victims of abuse, with the mean age between six and nine (Dumas, 1992). According to the National Center on Child Abuse Prevention, reported cases of child abuse rose 147 percent between 1979 and 1989, and cases continue to rise. Sexual abuse accounted for 15 to 16 percent of those reports (Dumas, 1992).

> **VOICES OF EXPERIENCE**
>
> *"Nobody who has not been in the interior of a family can say what the difficulties of any individual of that family may be."*
> —Jane Austen, author

Other than the direct correlations to lack of success in school, what are some effects of child abuse?

_____

_____

_____

Children who have suffered abuse often lose their sense of self-esteem. Many children who become runaways, teenage prostitutes, prison inmates, and suicides have been victims of child abuse. Though some children are able to recover from their experiences, others are affected for the rest of their lives (Greenberg, 1994).

If you have reason to believe that a student in your class has been abused, it is important for you to take appropriate action. Be sure to follow your school's policy and the laws of your state regarding child abuse. In some states you will be required to report suspected child abuse; in some locations it may suffice to report the evidence to a school counselor or to your principal. To take no action may be inviting disaster for the child and may, depending upon the laws in your state, be illegal.

Government advisor on family policy Richard Weissbourd has pointed out that in many cases economic stresses in the family play a significant role in a child's school life (Weissbourd, 1996). What do you think might be some economic stresses on children of families who are poor?

_____

_____

Weissbourd says that children from poor families may need to work to earn money for the family, care for adult relatives, or provide child care for a younger sibling. He cited a survey of high school students which showed that about 20 percent of students reported having missed days of school so that they could care for a family member or close friend. In 1992, according to Weissbourd, "12 percent of high school dropouts nationwide reported that they had to care for a family member and 11 percent said that they had to help financially support their families (these groups overlap, since respondents could answer yes to more than one question)" (Weissbourd, 1996, p. 27).

A family may face additional challenges or frustrations when one of its members stands out as being "different" in some way. One member may join a different political party, may exhibit mental illness, may choose a different religion, may behave differently, may have a different sexual orientation, or may be born with or acquire a disability. Still, there are many common ties that can unite family members as they learn to embrace diversity and eventually benefit from it.

> **VOICES OF EXPERIENCE**
>
> *"The family only represents one aspect, however important an aspect, of a human being's functions and activities.... A life is beautiful and ideal, or the reverse, only when we have taken into our consideration the social as well as the family relationship."*
> *–Havelock Ellis, psychologist and writer*

Turnbull & Turnbull (1990) explained that the process of accepting an exceptional family member may be similar to that of accepting the death of a loved one. However, if long-term planning, empowerment and advocacy, community integration, and financial planning are taken into consideration, the grief can be turned into something positive. Feelings of grief may arise in times of stress. Families may grieve for the child they have and for the child that might have been. They may grieve for relationships that are permanently changed. Or they may grieve for themselves and for some imagined ideal life. The process may include any of the following emotions: shock, depression, isolation, denial, guilt, shame, anger, fear, uncertainty, and acceptance.

No family can be without diversity because every individual is unique. When the members of the family realize this fact, they tend to embrace differences and to view them as enriching opportunities for growth rather than as challenges or problems. However, it is often the case that some members of a family feel strongly about their traditional religion, ethnicity, politics, or lifestyle. These individuals may go through a process of adjustment and acceptance which can best be aided by education.

The reason that diversity is a positive aspect of society is that fear of the unfamiliar inhibits the exchange of ideas and the cooperation which promotes enlightenment and the advance of humankind. The experience of diversity among those whom we love best motivates us to give up our fear and to move forward. Therefore, all of society benefits from our familial feeling.

TERMINOLOGY    The following concepts need to be considered when thinking about family issues in the classroom:

**Child Abuse.** This is any behavior that hurts a child physically or emotionally.

**Circle of friends.** This refers to the many people whose lives overlap ours. We have an inner circle of relatives, bonded by family ties. A second circle includes close friends. Third, we have casual acquaintances. Finally, we have those who are paid to be in our lives, such as our teachers, doctors, and employers.

**Disabled Abuse.** This refers to abuse of individuals with disabilities, including neglect.

**Domestic Abuse.** This refers to the abuse of one family member by another.

**Emotional Abuse.** This includes using words or withholding affection to hurt someone.

**Extended families.** This is a family of several generations living together in the home, possibly including aunts and uncles.

**Latchkey Kids.** This refers to children who spend longer than three hours at home every day without adult supervision.

**Migrant family.** This is a family which has relocated to a new country and faces the burden of cultural change along with other adjustments. It may also be a family which faces many changes resulting from constant movement due to employment opportunities.

**Neglect.** This involves failing to give a child, person with a disability, or elderly adult proper shelter, food, clothing, or health care (Greenberg, 1994).

**Nontraditional family.** Families made up of adults who are cohabiting, same-gender partners, single parents, and their children are called nontraditional, though they are rapidly growing in number.

**Nuclear family.** This is a family consisting of two generations in the home, parents and their children. Nuclear families include one-parent and adoptive families.

**Reorganized family.** This is a family which has been created through marriage, remarriage, or cohabitation of people who had children by former partners.

**Sexual Abuse.** This type of behavior ranges from obscene phone calls and indecent exposure to rape (Greenberg, 1994).

**Throwaways.** These are children who are either forced out of their homes or abandoned by their parents (Greenberg, 1994).

**Verbal Abuse.** This involves using cruel language and insults to hurt someone (Greenberg, 1994).

EMPOWERMENT TIPS

Here are some tips to help improve your interactions with students from diverse family situations.

❦ *Remember that your knowledge of your students is limited.* Though you spend several hours a day in their company, you probably know very little of their family situations, the neighborhoods in which they live, and sometimes even their physical health. While your assessments must be based on your own observations, grades, attendance, and classroom behavior, consider what factors may contribute to any problems you see.

❦ *Be aware of signs of abuse.* These include: spontaneous statements made by the child; precocious sex play or talk, infantile or aggressive behavior, uncharacteristic cheerfulness, secretiveness or vigilance, and sudden changes in mood or action. Be aware that any of these signs may also occur where there is no abuse, so be alert but don't to jump to conclusions (Dumas, 1992).

- *Do whatever is appropriate to know the parents or guardians of your students.* Talk on the phone. Invite them to school.

- *When speaking with parents, always have something positive to say.* First discuss the qualities in the child you can praise. Then discuss any problems.

- *Call parents when something is going well.* Let them know of accomplishments and progress so that you are not associated with negative conditions.

CLASSROOM STRATEGIES

The following classroom strategies will prove useful in fostering communication among families, students, and teachers.

- Offer evening activities and conference times so that working parents can be more actively involved in the child's school life. If evening meetings are not possible, stay in close communication via telephone and e-mail.

- Share with parents your teaching strategies, and keep them informed of your approach to teaching their child. Involve parents by seeking their assistance and forming a partnership for your common goal to educate their child. Remember to think of parents as your staff of teaching assistants.

- When parents are upset, wait for a brief cooling-off period before meeting with them. Calm down yourself by postponing conversations for a few minutes before you see them. A confrontational manner offers no positive outcome. If parents are upset, do not meet with them in an isolated area of the school. Meet in the office area, and have another professional present if at all possible.

- Don't feel that you must be all things to the parents of your students. You are the teacher, not the principal, social worker, counselor, or nurse. Do not hesitate to refer parents to appropriate help when it is needed.

- Encourage the development of school guidelines about appropriate involvement with noncustodial parents, the involvement of stepparents and cohabiting adults in school activities, and other matters pertaining to nontraditional families (adapted from Weissbourd, 1996).

- Eliminate from your language the idea that one kind of family is more legitimate or superior to another. Keep in mind that every family is different.

Finally, let's return to the scenario that opened this chapter. Read the situation below and record your reactions. Answering the questions will help prepare you to handle family issues in the classroom. There is no one "right" answer, so be thoughtful and be yourself.

|  |  |
|---|---|
| Setting: | Your classroom |
| Time: | During a regularly scheduled parent conference |
| Person involved: | Mr. and Mrs. Kaplan (parents of Anna, you student) |
| Background: | Mr. and Mrs. Kaplan have been supportive, pleasant parents whom you have come to know quite well, or so you thought. |
| Circumstances: | The Kaplans asked for this conference to discuss a problem they are having. |
| Simulation: | After briefly discussing Anna's good performance in your class, Mr. Kaplan asks for your advice on a very serious problem. He says he and his wife are getting a divorce. Their concern is with whom Anna should live. They each want Anna. Anna told her parents she would go with the one you recommend. They then ask for your recommendation. |

1. What is your objective?

_____

_____

_____

2. What will you say to the Kaplans?

_____

_____

_____

3. What will you say to Anna?

_____

_____

_____

**CONCLUSION**  We must stay aware that when we feel powerless to fix problems, sometimes we stop seeing them altogether. Left unattended, however, these problems grow into devastating school failure, which leads to such things as alienation, dropping out of school, drug abuse, and long-term welfare dependency. While teachers may not be able to make dramatic changes, we can fix upon small deeds which make a significant difference in a child's life and prospects for a positive future. We can help to secure glasses for a child with vision impairment, find school supplies for a child who is in need, and stay aware of the pervasive threats to children's learning (Weissbourd, 1996).

Though families are the source and the center of children's lives, we must also remember that children do not exist in a vacuum. As Weissbourd (1996) pointed out, children "are not merely products of advantaged or disadvantaged home environments—they are not putty in their parents' hands—they are powerfully shaped by a vast array of circumstances in the larger world" (p. 27). We must go beyond the stereotypes of race, class, and family income if we are ever to effectively address the problems which afflict our students and so profoundly affect their ability to learn.

REFERENCES

Cushner, K., McClelland, A., & Safford, P. (1996). *Human diversity in education: An integrative approach.* New York: McGraw-Hill.

Dumas, L. S. (1992). *Talking with your child about a troubled world.* New York: Fawcett Columbine.

Dwinell, L. & Baetz, R. (1993). *We did the best we could: How to create healing between the generations.* Deerfield Beach, FL: Health Communications, Inc.

Greenberg, K. (1994). *Family abuse: Why do people hurt each other?* New York: Twenty-first Century Books.

Seufert-Barr, N. (1994). Families around the world: Universal in their diversity. *UN Chronicle, 31,* 46.

Turnbull, A. P. & Turnbull, H. R. (1990). *Families, professionals, and exceptionality: A special partnership.* Columbus, OH: Merrill.

Weissbourd, R. (1996). *The vulnerable child: What really hurts America's children and what we can do about it.* Reading, MA: Addison-Wesley Publishing Company.

# The Laws of Human Diversity

15

By the end of this chapter you should be able to answer these questions:

- What do we mean by educational rights?
- What are the specific educational rights of diverse learners?
- What are some laws which guarantee educational opportunities for students with disabilities?
- How can teachers help to educate students and their families about their legal rights?

THE CLASSROOM IS
A MICROCOSM

*Y*ou are doing some grading at your desk just prior to the first bell when Cassie, one of your highest academic achievers, shyly approaches and asks to speak to you about a problem. At your nod, she quickly states the following: "You always call on the boys instead of the girls, even when we have our hands raised. I counted last week, and you called on boys ten times for every two you called on a girl. I think you like boys better. It's not fair. My mother said it's gender discrimination."

INTRODUCTION

*W*e have seen in the preceding chapters that classroom teachers encounter diversity at every turn. Human diversity falls into many categories, and the social climate in a culture tends to affect a number of aspects at once. In other words, interest in promoting the rights of all people in general leads to attention to the rights of specific groups.

Today, all students in the United States are legally entitled to a free and appropriate education. This was not always true in the past. Can you list some categories of individuals who were previously excluded or ignored?

_____

_____

_____

In the past we have ignored such students as those who

---

**Human diversity is
protected on three levels:**

- **Local**  ☑
- **State**  ☑
- **Federal**  ☑

---

were not legal citizens of the United States, those with disabilities, and those whose first language was not English.

How teachers behave in the classroom today reflects decades and even centuries of changing attitudes and increased awareness and information about the human condition. Changes in our legal, moral, and social attitudes have come from many directions. Can you think of some examples of sources of change in our laws?

_____

_____

_____

In the United States, the labor movements of the 1930s helped to focus some attention on physical impediments to work. Child labor abuses drew attention to the needs and rights of children. The 1950s and 60s saw the beginning of the civil rights movement, which focused on the need for social change in regard to African Americans. How did the civil rights movement help the plight of all Americans, and ultimately bring change to our schools?

_____

_____

_____

The civil rights movement helped bring positive change to our schools because of our gradual realization that the methods which proved effective in raising the consciousness of the American people about the plight of African Americans could be successfully implemented to improve rights in other areas of society. Can you name some areas where these methods were implemented?

_____

_____

_____

The concept of equal rights to appropriate and free education for every child came to be recognized, as well as specific rights for diverse individuals. It is impossible to guarantee the right to equal opportunity in education without respecting all areas of diversity. Name some other

210

rights which must be guaranteed in order to insure equal education:

_____

_____

_____

In order to benefit equally from schooling, all children must be guaranteed freedom from discrimination based upon gender, sexual orientation, disability, race, ethnicity, language, socioeconomic status, or learning difference.

PERSPECTIVE
ONE

While we work in our classrooms to promote the fundamental changes in individual and societal attitudes which will encourage understanding and tolerance of difference, it is important to protect human and civil rights through legislation as well.  In what ways are those rights protected now?

_____

_____

_____

Local, state, and federal laws insure educational opportunities, provide for appropriate education and medical care, and seek to secure access to public buildings and streets for every child.

The following is a brief discussion of some major areas of legislative protection.  It is important for every teacher to be aware of the laws protecting students' rights.  Even a cursory study of this chapter will help you to see some of the difficulties students with exceptionalities may encounter, and should raise your consciousness and increase your awareness of the ways in which children can be unfairly penalized in the classroom for being different.

Students have benefited from laws respecting diversity in general, and specifically from laws protecting their civil rights and guaranteeing freedom from discrimination based on disabilities.  However, there has been no legislation

> **VOICES OF EXPERIENCE**
>
> *"The great law of culture is: Let each become all that he was created capable of being; expand, if possible, to his full growth; resisting all impediments . . . and show himself at length in how own shape and stature, be these what they may."*
> *—Thomas Carlyle, scholar*

passed to protect a student's right to other characteristics of diversity, such as those relating to sexual orientation, gender, or learning differences. There have been legal tests of some of these issues, however, and the court decisions in those cases are beginning to form the legislative boundaries within which school systems must operate. Can you think of any court cases which have influenced current school guidelines?

_____

_____

_____

One famous case was *Brown vs. the Board of Education of Topeka, Kansas* (1954). There the court determined that racially segregated schools were separate but not equal in terms of educational opportunities for all students. Another case, *Plyer vs. Doe* (1982), was decisive in its determination of educational entitlements for children who are not legal residents of the United States.

PERSPECTIVE
TWO

Teachers are not expected to be lawyers, and it is not necessary to know the particulars of legislation regarding students' rights and school responsibilities. It is, however, useful to be familiar in general with some of the more important laws pertaining to schools and schooling. Following are some examples:

1) The Rehabilitation Act of 1973 provides for a "Barrier-Free Environment" for people with disabilities and defines these individuals as persons who have a physical or mental impairment which substantially limits one or more major activities, have a record of such an impairment, or are regarded as having such an impairment. The Act requires any program or activity receiving federal monies to provide equal access and opportunities for people with disabilities. This includes people with cancer, heart disease, diabetes; cerebral palsy, epilepsy, mental illness, mental retardation; muscular dystrophy, multiple sclerosis; drug addiction and alcoholism; visual, hearing, and communication disorders. This comprehensive Act affects state and local government, education, transportation, housing, and employment.

2) The Americans with Disabilities Act (ADA) of 1990 (Public Law 101-336) is considered a "civil rights bill" for individuals with disabilities.

212

The ADA grants civil rights protection to individuals with disabilities in all public services, public accommodations, transportation, and telecommunications. Public accommodations affected by the ADA include such facilities as hotels, restaurants, auditoriums, stores, banks, doctors' offices, museums, libraries, parks, zoos, schools, and recreation facilities. According to ADA, it is discriminatory to fail to remove structural, architectural, and communication barriers in facilities where such removal is readily achievable.

3) The Individuals with Disabilities Education Act (IDEA), formerly the Education of All Handicapped Children Act, became law in 1990. Its purpose is to guarantee the availability of special education programs to children and youth with disabilities and to assure that educational decisions relating to such students are fair and appropriate. Additionally, it assists state and local governments in providing special education through the use of federal funds. It requires schools to provide appropriate elementary and secondary education to children and youth ages 3-22. This public law has been amended several times and now includes the provision of services for adolescents who are leaving school programs and beginning adult life, and requires the educational program of a student with a disability to include a plan for transition to post-secondary life. This plan must include appropriate assistive technology which benefits the student, such as microcomputers, alternative speech devices, and keyboards.

PERSPECTIVE
THREE

In addition to specific legislation such as that discussed above, there are legal definitions which every teacher, and, indeed, every citizen would do well to know and understand. Some examples follow.

*Equal Protection.* Equal Protection of the Law means that everyone has a Constitutional right to receive the same protection under state law as any other person. The 14th Amendment to the Constitution says that "No State shall ... deny to any person within its jurisdiction the equal protection of the laws." Discuss some of the reasons this protection is necessary. Can you think of ways in which children have suffered discrimination in schools in the past?

_____

_____

Equal Protection of Laws was meant to prevent state governments from favoring particular groups of people at the expense of other groups. All people are protected, including the poor, children, prisoners, non-citizens, and minorities. State constitutions also contain equal protection clauses.

*Child Advocacy.* The public policy decisions which have the greatest impact on children and families are made at the state and local levels. Child advocacy organizations speak out for improvement in the condition of the children in their community and state through legislative, executive, and judicial decisions on programs to meet children's needs. These issues and decisions directly affect school law. What concerns do you imagine child advocates need to address?

_____

_____

Child advocates focus on basic income and family support, child welfare, juvenile justice, nutrition, education, and child care programs.

How would you define the term "family"?

_____

_____

The term "family" does not have a precise legal meaning, so most laws include a definition of the term when they use it. In some legislation, the term means only people who are related by blood or marriage and live together. In other laws, family includes relatives who may or may not live in the same household. In still other laws it can mean two people or a group of people who stay committed to one another in a domestic setting for an unlimited period of time, sharing a home and responsibility for financial support and household duties. No specific number of persons is necessary to make up a legal family (Leonard, 1990)

*Race and Nationality.* In one generation we have seen extraordinary progress toward full integration and equality for all races and nationalities in our schools. Can you think of some examples, either personal or public, which illustrate changes in our national attitudes regarding race discrimination?

_____

_____

_____

One example is Charlayne Hunter (Gault), who became familiar to television viewers across America when, as a child, she had to be protected by the National Guard from protesters as she integrated a southern school. Today, Ms. Gault is widely known as a national public television news anchor.

*Educational Opportunity.* People of all different ethnic, racial, and national origins now have legal protection from educational discrimination (Coughlin, 1993). The 14th Amendment to the Constitution states that it is illegal to classify a citizen by his or her national origin, since a foreigner is entitled to equal protection under the law once that individual has been naturalized as a citizen. Another ground-breaking law was Brown v. Board of Education (1954) which established as a matter of law that racially segregated education was unequal. Additionally, Title VII of the 1964 Civil Rights Act prohibits discrimination based upon an employee's race, color, or national origin.

*Religion.* Another major area of concern in schools is religion. The U.S. Constitution guarantees that all Americans are free to follow the religion of their choice or none at all. Briefly identify the basis of this guarantee of religious freedom:

_____

_____

Article I of the Bill of Rights states that "Congress shall make no law respecting an establishment of religion, or prohibiting the free exercise thereof." The government can neither establish a state religion nor force anyone to attend or support any religious institution. Individuals have the right to worship as they please.

> **VOICES OF EXPERIENCE**
>
> *"The people's good is the highest law."*
> —Cicero, Roman statesman

Although we may follow the letter of the law in our schools and classrooms, as individual teachers we also need to be aware of the spirit of the law. Looking at the religious-based wars and dissension around the world, we may congratulate ourselves on our right to religious freedom. However, though they are protected by laws, many students continue to suffer from a subtle bias against certain religions. What are some ways that religious bias may have an impact in the classroom?

_____

_____

_____

It is important to be sensitive to the fact that children may feel discriminated against when certain holidays are celebrated in school. For example, many public schools in the United States celebrate Christmas in some way, if only by taking a school vacation, while Jewish, Moslem, Buddhist, Hindu, and other minority religions may be hardly acknowledged, if at all. Such oversights may have a significant effect on the way our children perceive the importance of these religions, and therefore of the school's, the teacher's, and the community's attitude toward them and their beliefs.

*Sexual Orientation.* As of the publication of this worktext, no well-defined body of law guarantees the rights of students who are homosexual. No federal law protects gay and lesbian students from discrimination. Advocacy groups continue to focus on combating state-by-state anti-gay ballot initiatives, challenging the military ban, and establishing legal precedents to secure constitutional protection for all citizens. Brainstorm some reasons for securing protection under the law for students who are homosexual:

_____

_____

_____

As long as being homosexual is considered illegal, there can be no secure and lasting legal rights for all people (Cohen, 1994). Because our laws still don't protect equal rights on the basis of sexual orientation, students who are gay, lesbian, or bisexual continue to face discriminatory practices. It should also be recognized that people who are heterosexual also have no legal protection on the basis of their sexual orientation.

*Size and Stature.* As of the publication of this textbook, no well-defined body of law guarantees the rights of students who are overweight or excessively tall or short. Advocacy groups seek to fight discrimination against people on the basis of weight or stature. They work to educate lawmakers and serve as national legal clearinghouses for attorneys challenging size discrimination. Can you think of ways in which children who are abnormally short, tall, or overweight might suffer in the classroom because of their differences?

_____

_____

_____

The inaccessibility of public facilities is problematic for those who may not find ample legroom, headroom, or seating space in public transportation, theatres, schools, and other such places.

This overview of laws concerning diversity is merely an introduction. Educators need to understand the law in order to:

- Avoid legal problems
- Know their own and their students' legal rights
- Understand the language of the law
- Know how to report a violation of rights
- Know what constitutes a crime
- Avoid becoming the victim of a crime

PERSPECTIVE
FOUR

As we have become educated as a culture about the causes and effects of exceptionalities, and have learned to value diversity, we have made some significant, though still inadequate, progress in the development of legal protection of human rights. Through that legislation we have begun to undergo real social change. Clearly, the most vital arena for this change is our classrooms. Teachers are among the many unsung heroes of change. As models of tolerance and vigilant protectors and champions of the rights of their students they have done much to move our society forward. Do you have heroes of change? List a few below and tell what they have done to secure freedom for our future generations:

_____

_____

_____

_____

Countless individuals have sacrificed time, money, energy, and sometimes their lives to bring about legislative change. For example, civil rights leaders Martin Luther King, Jr. and Madger Evers gave their lives for racial justice. Rosa Parks risked her life for integration of public transportation. Col. Margarethe Cammermeyer revealed her sexual orientation at the risk of her military career. Vietnam war veteran Ron Kovic dedicated his life to securing the rights of veterans with disabilities. Madeline Murray O'Hair, an atheist, fought for her freedom *not* to worship.

As time passes, new issues arise which demand attention and resolution. In the 1980s and 90s, a major new source of concern was

217

the question of how to meet the needs of children with AIDS and other contagious diseases while protecting all students and respecting all their rights. Also of concern are the problems of drug abuse as they have an impact on the rules we set within our schools and our classrooms. Other controversial issues in education include:

- ethnic history and literature
- sex education
- values
- gender studies
- minority studies
- observance of religious holidays
- school prayer
- bias in standardized testing
- bilingual education
- inclusion

EMPOWERMENT
TIPS

Here are some tips to help you ensure the legal rights of your students.

- *It is crucial that all individuals involved in the classroom feel a link with the teacher.* Make family members feel connected to you, and let administrators know that you are adhering to the rules. Students need to know that they can trust you to advocate for their rights.

- *Invite members of local advocacy groups to speak to your classes, as age appropriateness dictates.* This will educate students about the issues as well as inform them about being self-advocates.

- *Create an open atmosphere in your classroom.* Make sure your students feel comfortable telling you if they believe their rights have been violated.

- *Encourage parents and guardians to let you know if they are dissatisfied with any classroom situations or academic content.* You may be able to answer their concerns yourself, or refer them to the appropriate administrator.

Finally, let's return to the scenario that opened this chapter. Read the situation below and record your reactions. Answering the questions will help prepare you to handle legal issues in the classroom. There is no one "right" answer, so be thoughtful and be yourself.

|  |  |
|---|---|
| Setting: | Your classroom |
| Time: | Just prior to the first bell |
| Person involved: | Cassie, one of your students |
| Background: | Cassie is a high academic achiever. |
| Circumstances: | Cassie approaches your desk and asks to speak to you about a problem. |
| Simulation: | Cassie quickly states the following: "You always call on the boys instead of the girls, even when we have our hands raised. I counted last week, and you called on boys ten times for every two you called on a girl. I think you like boys better. It's not fair. My mother said it's gender discrimination." |

1. What is your objective?

_____

_____

_____

2. What do you say to Cassie?

_____

_____

_____

3. What will you say to Cassie's mother?

_____

_____

_____

Many challenges remain in the attempt to secure full participation in society for each and every person regardless of race, gender, religion, sexual orientation, ethnicity, age, or disabling condition. It will take the continued efforts of dedicated individuals to bring about more change, and fundamental change will occur in the classrooms of our country. Teachers have been, and will remain, on the frontlines of the battle for legal protection of the rights of all children.

References

Cohen, D. G. (1994). The rights of gay men and lesbians. *Legal Interest*, 5-10.

Coughlin, G. G. (1993). *Your handbook of everyday law.* New York: Harper Perennial.

Leonard, R. (1990). *Family law dictionary.* Berkeley, CA: Nolo Press.

# Making a Difference in Society

**OBJECTIVES**

By the end of this chapter you should be able to:

🍎 Develop your own strategies for assisting students in dealing with diverse individuals.

🍎 Begin to alter biased attitudes children learn from their parents and from other adults in society.

🍎 Establish yourself as a role model for your students and peers.

**THE CLASSROOM IS A MICROCOSM**

*Your first job as a teacher is an unexpected challenge. Your students all look remarkably alike, and you have trouble distinguishing between them and remembering their names. Though there is no dress code at your school, your students all dress alike and have the same hair style. Group work proves unproductive because no one seems to have an original idea. Class discussions fall flat because no one ever has a different perspective. Grading homework is tedious because everyone's answers are identical. You begin to doubt your abilities to create a vibrant classroom . . . but then you wake up, relieved to realize that it was just a nightmare!*

**INTRODUCTION**

Although it appears that people have generally become more understanding of human differences over the past several decades, and though we have attempted to institutionalize respect for human difference through legislation, it is still common for individuals to fear and ridicule those who are different. For instance, someone may be critical of a person with a visible disability who eats in a restaurant. Another person may be concerned about a group living home for people who are diverse being established in his or her neighborhood. Prejudice against a co-worker because of race, gender, or sexual orientation is something many of us hear expressed on a regular basis. Myths and negative attitudes about human diversity still exist, and will exist until we change them, one person at a time. The easiest person to change is the one you see when you look in the mirror. We hope that this course has been a good beginning for you.

"Every bigot was once a child free of prejudice."
—Sister Mary de Lourdes

There has been progress toward establishing equal rights for diverse people. However, that does not mean that everyone who interacts with them will be kind, considerate, or comfortable. Part of the problem is that children learn certain attitudes from their parents and from other adults and peers in society. Now you are in a position to alter those attitudes for yourself and others. You are equipped with information and can help to insure that society makes additional progress beyond the laws which have assisted people who are diverse.

Wouldn't you prefer to live in a society where people don't stare at others who are different? Where everyone, regardless of race, ethnic, or religious background, gender, sexual orientation, age, intellectual ability, nationality, socioeconomic level, size, or shape is treated with respect? Where people are evaluated on the basis of their skills and their personality, not on the basis of the labels which have been imposed upon them? When that happens, the society is richer in every way because we all have the opportunity to contribute to the fullest extent of our capacity. You have the ability now to influence others so that fair treatment is afforded to everyone.

This final chapter will help you to develop strategies for assisting others in dealing with diverse individuals. Remember that you are educated now. By taking this course, you have prepared yourself to be a leader of others, and others will follow your example since they know you have had an opportunity to study and consider these issues. Each of the sections in this chapter offers you ideas and encouragement as you reconsider your own attitudes and begin to change society. It will be a wonderful and exciting experience to grow in understanding as you help others to do the same!

PERSPECTIVE ONE
Each chapter has stressed the importance of being comfortable when you interact with people who are different. Comfort logically follows the reduction of fear as you dispel myths, correct misinformation, and develop knowledge and understanding. Some steps toward becoming more comfortable around people who are different are listed below.

- Make a firm personal decision to be comfortable when you interact with anyone different from you. Often, merely having the *intention* to be comfortable will help you to actually feel comfortable. You might begin your day with an affirmation such as this: "Today I hope to meet someone different from me so that I can discover an underlying similarity."

- Continue to learn more about human diversity. Consider taking additional courses. Classes which offer skills such as sign language will make it possible for you to easily converse with people who use that form of communication and will make you a more expressive person. Showing an interest in the problems of any special interest group, whether it is a senior citizens' organization, a women's rights group, a local AIDS service organization, or a club for international students, will broaden your perspective and allow you to participate more fully in the world. At your college or in your neighborhood you should be able to find many opportunities for interacting with different types of people.

♦ When you make friends with people who are different, don't be afraid to talk to them about their exceptionality. Ask the questions you want to ask. Raise the issues you want to raise. Openness and honesty is the key to friendship, and it is important to treat people who are different the same way you treat anyone else. Remember that the most important lesson you have learned is that individuals are unique. They are not defined by labels.

♦ Assist different types of people through volunteer organizations. This will offer you another opportunity to get to know people with differences. Literacy programs exist in every community, as do programs for economically disadvantaged people, and nearly every other category of exceptionality. Such organizations or agencies will welcome your assistance and will usually have a variety of projects or activities from which you can choose. An annotated listing of organizations dealing with human diversity is included in the appendix of this book.

♦ Include diverse people among your acquaintances and friends. Don't be afraid to invite someone different to social functions. Remember that differences are not contagious, and even if they were, you and every other person alive is exceptional in some way, in some context. Some of your friends may not be comfortable with your new acquaintance. Their response may be due to their ignorance, and you can use that as an opportunity to help them see your perspective.

♦ Just be yourself around people who are different. If you are false, they will recognize it. Don't worry about your mood—we all have good and bad days. Don't adjust your vocabulary. Consider the feelings of others as you always do, letting your new knowledge and sensitivity enhance your natural good manners.

PERSPECTIVE
TWO

Now, or in the future, you may be in the position of having significant influence upon your community. In addition to teaching young people, you may belong to civic, religious, and professional organizations. You may become a leader in your field and have responsibility for hiring or influencing the careers of others. What wonderful opportunities you may have to make a positive impact upon our society.

As a member of a civic, religious, or professional group, you certainly can set an example for others regarding interactions with diverse people. Some individuals with exceptionalities may need your sponsorship to facilitate their membership, or they may need special accommodations for access in order to participate fully.

For instance, if your group is presenting a special speaker and opening the meeting to the public, be sure to hire a sign language interpreter and let that be known in your publicity so that those needing that service will be motivated to attend. Obvious requirements when selecting a location for a meeting, such as wheelchair ramps, may be overlooked by those unaccustomed to thinking inclusively. You can point out these considerations.

If you become active in politics, you will have many chances to significantly influence the funding of programs, the establishment of procedures for service development and provision, and the design of laws which directly affect diverse people. At the local, state, and federal level, as an active politician or simply as a voter, you should follow two simple rules. The first is that people who are different deserve every opportunity to lead the normal lives they desire. The second is that they should not be merely tolerated or accepted, but respected as full and important members of the community.

PERSPECTIVE TWO

Before closing your study of human diversity you might consider your future. You obviously care about education, but how will you focus your unique talents? Such specialized fields as psychology, sociology, anthropology, political science, counseling, medicine, special education, music therapy, speech and language therapy, sheltered workshop management, sign language interpreting, and many others offer challenging careers which let you make meaningful contributions to your fellow citizens. If you think you might be interested, a good way to begin is to visit some professionals in the area of your choice to explore the possibilities and ask advice on some courses of study.

PERSPECTIVE THREE

Now that you are educated and informed about human diversity, here is a test of your new attitudes and ability to respect and assist those who are considered different. Imagine this situation:

You are being wheeled into a hospital emergency room. You have sustained a life-threatening injury. Your life depends upon the ability of the lone doctor on duty. Which *one* of the labels in the chart below do you want that doctor to have? Circle your choice.

*Male   Female   Christian   Jewish   Homosexual   Heterosexual*

*Slim   Tall   Heavy   Short   Wealthy   Disabled   Caucasian   Hindu*

*Black   Hispanic   Old   Young   Foreign   Poor   Muslim   Expert*

If you value your life, more than likely your answer was "Expert." It is doubtful that you would refuse treatment and choose to die if the doctor had any of the other labels coupled with "expert." Since that is true, we know that you, and most everyone else, can ignore labels when it suits our needs. If you can choose to ignore them at all times and in all situations, looking only at the abilities of the person involved, then you have learned to treat individuals with the respect they deserve. When old habits of thinking and fears based on prejudice and ignorance creep in, it is a handy reminder to ask yourself, "If I were in that hospital emergency room and this person were the only doctor on duty, would I want this person to save my life?" Every time you say "yes," you save your own humanity and make the world a much better place.

CONCLUSION

Your study of human diversity is at a close. The next step you take is up to you. We hope that this text has inspired you to continue discovering more about differences among people. We are confident that you are now equipped to make a difference in the lives of people with whom you come in contact. We are also confident that you can set an example in your classroom and community. As you strive to learn more about human diversity, we hope that you continue to see the underlying unity among all peoples while at the same time you respect individual uniqueness. The human race has a long way to go before universal understanding becomes the norm, but the only way we'll ever reach that goal is by changing one person at a time, starting with ourselves. If, after this course, you have a better understanding of human diversity and an attitude of respect for persons who are diverse, you have taken a big step toward the goal.

# Appendices: Resources for the Classroom

Appendix A:  Nondiscrimination Policy
*Adopt this policy for your own classroom, or use it as a model for your students to write their own.*

Appendix B:  Suggested Readings
*The diverse books and articles listed here will broaden your perspectives and enrich your appreciation for human diversity.*

Appendix C:  National Diversity Programs and Services
*The organizations, services, and Internet homepages listed here provide further information on the topics covered in this worktext.*

# Nondiscrimination Policy

As fellow members of the human race, this classroom supports the diversity of students, staff, and parents who make up the stakeholders of our school.

Current nondiscrimination policies and practices of our school district already support and celebrate this diversity.

To demonstrate our unity in diversity, we will not accept any kind of prejudicial, obscene, demeaning, abusive, or profane language, gestures, or acts.

# Suggested Readings

Angelou, M. (1989). *I know why the caged-bird sings.* New York: Literacy Volunteers of New York City.
*This is the autobiography of an African-American woman, telling how she overcame the social biases of growing up poor and black to become a fully realized and successful person.*

Brown, C. (1976). *The children of ham.* New York: Stein and Day.

*This book offers personal accounts of African-American youth in the slums of Harlem and their proposed solution to their social ills.*

Duval, L. (1994). Respecting our differences: A guide to getting along in a changing world. Minneapolis, MN: Free Spirit.
*Discussions of accepting, respecting, and celebrating differences are provided in this guide.*

Frank, A. (1956). *The diary of Anne Frank.* New York: Random House.

*A young Jewish girl's spirit triumphs in the face of Nazi occupation, just before she and her family are exterminated on the basis of their race and religion.*

Gerbner, G. (1990). Communication. *Encyclopedia Americana* (International edition, vol. 7, pp. 423-24). Danbury, CT: Grolier.
*This is an insightful overview of the diverse ways in which humans exchange information.*

Gold, S. & Kibria, N. (1993). Vietnamese refugees and blocked mobility. *Asian and Pacific Migration Journal, 2*(1), 27-56.
*This journal examines data from published sources and ethnographic studies of the economic situation of Vietnamese refugees in the United States.*

Hirsch, E. D., Kett, J. F., & Trefil, J. (1988). *The Dictionary of Cultural Literacy.* Boston: Houghton Mifflin Co.
*This is an essential quick reference for facts and terminology relating to world literature, philosophy, religion, art, history, politics, geography, anthropology, sociology, psychology, science, mathematics, medicine, and technology.*

Jampolsky, G. G. (1990). *Love is the answer: Creating positive relationships.* New York: Bantam.

    *This is a guide to improving interpersonal relationships, love, and peace of mind.*

Keyes, K. (1990). *The living love way.* San Francisco: New Dimensions Foundation.

    *This book discusses the importance of transforming conflict in one's daily life and expressing love wherever and whenever possible. The discussion also provides insights about the possibilities of world peace.*

Kroeber, A. J. & Kluckhohn, C. (Eds.). (1954). *Culture: A critical review of concepts and definitions.* New York: Random House.

    *This is an invaluable overview of cultural concepts and definitions.*

Kronenwetter, M. (1993). *Prejudice in America: Causes and cures.* New York: Franklin Watts.

    *This book traces the origins of prejudice in America and suggests practical solutions to the far-reaching problem.*

Mindel, C. H. & Habenstein, R. W. (Eds.). (1988). Ethnic families in America: Patterns and variation (3rd ed.). New York: Elsevier Publications.

    *This book examines ethnic family strengths and needs as well as historical background and demographic characteristics.*

Momaday, N. S. (1990). *The way to rainy mountain.* Albuquerque: University of New Mexico Press.

    *This is an account of the legends of the Kiowa Indians and how their ancient religion and culture were suddenly and brutally eradicated.*

Monette, P. (1992). *Becoming a man: Half a life story.* New York: Harcourt Brace Jovanovich.

    *Provided in this autobiography are a gay man's poignant memories of growing up, coming out to his parents, and battling AIDS.*

Neusner, J. (1994). *World religions in America.* Louisville, KY: John Knox.

    *This book examines the faiths of African-Americans, Hispanics, Native Americans, and all other major denominations. It also examines the subjects of women and religion, politics and religion, and society and religion.*

Vedder, R & Gallaway, L. (1993). Declining black employment. *Society*, 30(5), 57-63.

*This article explores income inequality during declining African-American employment, examines current welfare systems, and suggests ways to improve the economic disadvantages of minority groups.*

# National Diversity
# Programs and Services

The following resources are categorized according to the chapters of this worktext. Inclusion here does not necessarily constitute endorsement.

## 1. General Human Diversity

 Our Diverse World Homepage
http://www.coe.ufl.edu/DiverseWorld/
This is an interactive website where people can learn about every category of human diversity in detail. The goal of this homepage is to unite young people so that together they can preserve, celebrate, and grow from their differences.

 Resisting Defamation
2530 Berryessa Road, No. 616
San Jose, CA 95132
408-995-6545
408-923-5836 fax
This group works toward eliminating any stereotypes, slander, libel, or crimes against persons from different ethnic groups.

 American Civil Liberties Union
132 W. 43rd Street
New York, NY 10036
212-944-9800
212-869-9065 fax
With 200 local groups, the ACLU champions the rights set forth in the Bill of Rights of the U.S. Constitution: freedom of speech, press, assembly, and religion; due process of law and fair trial; equality before the law regardless of race, color, sexual orientation, national origin, political opinion, or religious belief.

 Section of Individual Rights and Responsibilities
c/o American Bar Association
1800 M Street NW, South Lobby
Washington, DC 20036
202-331-2280
202-331-2220 fax
The Section concentrates on law and public policy as they relate to civil and constitutional rights, civil liberties, and human rights in the United States and internationally. Its projects include representation of the homeless, people with AIDS, and those facing capital sentences.

Unity-and-Diversity World Council
5521 Grosvenor Boulevard, Suite 22
Los Angeles, CA 90066-6915
310-577-1968
310-578-1028 fax
This group provides worldwide coordination for cultural, scientific, educational, and religious nonprofit organizations, businesses, and individuals. It fosters "the emergence of a new universal person and civilization based on unity and diversity among all peoples and all life." The Council seeks to aid in establishing a new, worldwide civilization based upon the reality of the whole person by applying the methods and discoveries of modern science coupled with the insights of religion, philosophy, and the arts.

 People to People International
501 E. Armour Boulevard
Kansas City, MO 64109
816-531-4701
816-561-7502 fax
http://www.ptp.org/
This is a multinational, nongovernmental, nonpolitical corporation of individuals communicating with each other through personal contact, letters, and travel. The group promotes international friendship and understanding.

 The Friendship Force
57 Forsythe Street NW, Suite 900
575 S. Tower
Atlanta, GA 30303
404-522-9490
404-688-6148 fax
With 250 regional groups, members in 42 countries promote global understanding through the "force of friendship." A group of citizens flies to a city in another nation to stay in private homes for an exchange period of approximately two weeks, exchanging a cross-section from each community, representative of occupation, race, age, and gender.

 Worldwide Friendship International
3749 Brice Run Road, Suite A
Randallstown, MD 21133
410-922-2795
410-922-2795 fax
This group bridges gap among people of all nations through correspondence, so that they can learn each other's culture, language, and values. Membership spans 127 countries and encompasses numerous traditions, creeds, colors, ages, and national origins.

● The Council for Exceptional Children
1920 Association Drive
Reston, VA 22091
703-620-3660
800-328-0272
This council advances the quality of education for all exceptional children and improves the conditions under which special educators work. The Council is divided into smaller divisions which address children with behavioral disorders, mental retardation, communication disorders, learning disabilities, physical disabilities, and visual impairments. It also addresses gifted children and culturally and linguistically diverse exceptional learners.


## 2. The Culture of Diversity

● Institute for World Understanding of Peoples, Cultures and Languages
939 Coast Boulevard, 19DE
La Jolla, CA 92037
619-454-0705
The Institute conducts scientific research in establishing methodology for the comparative study of all populations, cultures, and languages. It also studies world organizations, especially in regard to the future of world civilization.

● American Community Cultural Center Association
19 Foothills Drive
Pompton Plains, NJ 07444
201-835-2661
The Association encourages people in all communities to develop cultural centers for the purpose of presenting cultural possibilities for everyone, regardless of economic status or geographic location.

● Federation of American Cultural and Language Communities
666 11th Street NW, Suite 800
Washington, DC 20001
202-387-0600
This is a coalition of ethnic organizations representing Americans of Armenian, French, German, Hispanic, Hungarian, Italian, Japanese, Sicilian, Ukrainian, and Vietnamese descent. They work to address areas of common interest to America's ethnic communities. The group seeks to further the rights of ethnic Americans, especially their cultural and linguistic rights.

# 3. Racial and Ethnic Diversity

◄ National Association for Ethnic Studies
Arizona State University
Department of English
PO Box 870302
Tempe, AZ 85287-0302
602-965-2197
602-965-3451 fax
email: naesi@asuvm.inre.asu.edu
This Association promotes research, study, and curriculum design in the field of ethnic studies, especially Native American, Black, Chicano, Puerto Rican, and Asian American.

◄ International Committee Against Racism
150 W. 28th Street, Room 301
New York, NY 10001
212-255-3959
312-663-9742 fax
Regional Groups: 4. State Groups: 30. Local Groups: 28. The Committee is dedicated to fighting all forms of racism and to building a multiracial society. The group opposes racism in all its economic, social, institutional, and cultural forms and believes racism destroys not only those minorities that are its victims, but all people.

◄ American Society for Ethnohistory
Department of Anthropology
McGraw Hall, Cornell University
Ithaca, NY 14853
607-277-0109
This Department promotes and encourages original research relating to the cultural history of ethnic groups worldwide.

◄ National Rainbow Coalition
1700 K Street NW, Suite 800
Washington, D.C. 20006
202-728-1180
http://www.bin.com/assocorg/rainbow/rainbow.htm
This multiracial organization fosters social, racial, and economic justice.

# 4. Gender and Sexual Orientation

 National Organization for Women
1000 16th Street NW, Suite 700
Washington, DC 20036
202-331-0066
202-331-9002 (TTY)
State Groups: 50.  Local Groups: 800.  This organization consists of men
and women who support "full equality of women in truly equal
partnership with men."  The group seeks to end prejudice and
discrimination against women in government, industry, the professions,
churches, political parties, the judiciary, labor unions, education,
science, medicine, law, religion, and other fields.

 National Council of Women of the United States
777 United Nations Plaza
New York, NY 10017
212-697-1278
The Council works for the education, participation, and advancement of
women in all areas of society.  It serves as an information center and
clearinghouse for affiliated women's organizations.

 National Organization for Men
11 Park Place
New York, NY 10007
212-686-MALE
212-766-4030
818-791-0578 fax
Regional Groups: 26.  Local Groups: 30.  The members of this group,
men and women, are united in efforts to promote and advance the equal
rights of men in matters such as affirmative action programs, alimony,
child custody, men's health, child abuse, battered husbands, divorce,
educational benefits, military conscription, and veterans' benefits.

 National Congress for Men
4511 Marathon Heights
Adrian, MI 49221-9240
202-FATHERS
State Groups: 50.  Local Groups: 80.  This is a coalition of organizations
and individuals promoting fathers' rights, men's rights, and equality of
the sexes.  It advocates the validity of traditional male roles in the family
and society.

Association for the Sexually Harassed
860 Manatawna Avenue
Philadelphia, PA 19128-1113
215-482-3528
This organization sponsors educational programs for school children.

 National Gay and Lesbian Task Force
2320 17th Street NW
Washington, DC 20009
202-332-6483
The Task Force is dedicated to the elimination of prejudice against persons based on their sexual orientation. It assists other associations in working effectively with the homosexual community and engages in direct action for gay freedom and full civil rights.

 National Gay Youth Network
PO Box 846
San Francisco, CA 94101-0846
Regional Groups: 74. State Groups: 80. Local Groups: 94. With gay youth support groups, gay student unions, and other interested groups, this group serves as a networking resource for the exchange of information.

 Renaissance Education Association
987 Old Eagle School Road, Suite 719
Wayne, PA 19087
610-975-9119
This association provides support and information about gender issues, including crossdressing, transvestism, transsexualism, and other transgender behavior.

 Equal Rights Advocates
1663 Mission Street, Suite 550
San Francisco, CA 94103
415-621-0672
415-621-6744 fax
This is a public interest law center specializing in sex discrimination cases.

## 5. Religious Diversity

 National Legal Foundation
6477 College Park Square, Suite 306
Virginia Beach, VA 23464
800-424-4242
804-397-4242
804-420-0855 fax
The Foundation actively litigates in defense of First Amendment liberties, with special focus on religious freedom. It prepares briefs, educational materials, and other publications on church-state issues for lawyers, teachers, and interested individuals.

 National Interreligious Task Force
4724 Cedar Avenue
Philadelphia, PA 19143
215-729-4084
With 20 local groups, this organization sponsors workshops on human rights and religious liberty.

 Religion in American Life
2 Queenston Place, Room 200
Princeton, NJ 08540
800-428-8292
609-921-3639
609-921-0551 fax
Leaders from Protestant, Roman Catholic, Eastern Orthodox, Unitarian, Muslim, Jewish, and other groups sponsor programs that support the contributions religion makes in American life.

 Coalition for Religious Freedom
5817 Dawes Avenue
Alexandria, VA 22311-1114
This interreligious organization seeks to preserve First Amendment rights to protect free exercise of religion.

 Rockford Institute Center on Religion and Society
2275 Half Day Road, Suite 350
Deerfield, IL 60015
800-383-0680
708-317-8062
708-317-8141 fax
This interreligious research and educational organization focuses on issues of culture and religion in society.

Facets of Religion
http://sunfly.ub.uni-freiburg.de/religion/
This colorful and informative Internet homepage discusses all major
religions of the world in depth, providing links to other sites of interest.


## 6. Socioeconomic Diversity

 Coalition for Economic Survival
1296 N. Fairfax Avenue
Los Angeles, CA 90046
213-656-4410
The Coalition addresses the economic concerns of senior citizens and
low-income families, especially issues dealing with rent control, tenants'
rights, and affordable housing.

 Center for Community Change
1000 Wisconsin Avenue, NW
Washington, DC 20007
202-342-0519
415-982-0346 (San Francisco office)
202-342-1132 fax
The center assists community groups of urban and rural poor in making
positive changes in their communities. It focuses attention on national
issues dealing with human poverty and works to make government more
responsive to the needs of the poor.

 National Center for Children in Poverty
Columbia University School of Public Health
154 Haven Avenue
New York, NY 10032
212-927-8793
212-927-9162 fax
This organization works to strengthen programs that improve the health
and development of children living in poverty.


## 7. Physical Diversity

 Council on Size and Weight Discrimination
PO Box 305
Mount Marion, NY 12456
914-679-1209
The goal of this council is to influence public policy and opinion in order
to end oppression based on discriminatory standards of body weight,
size, or shape.

National Association to Advance Fat Acceptance
PO Box 188620
Sacramento, CA 95818
800-442-1214
916-558-6880
916-558-6881 fax
Local chapters: 50. This association is dedicated to improving the quality of life for people who are fat by working to eliminate discrimination based on body size and provide people who are fat with the tools for self-empowerment through public education, advocacy, and member support. The group disseminates information about the sociological, psychological, legal, medical, and physiological aspects of being fat.

 Little People of America
7238 Piedmont Drive
Dallas, TX 75227-9324
800-24-DWARF
214-388-9576
Regional groups: 12. Local groups: 50. This group provides fellowship, interchange of ideas, moral support, and solutions to unique problems of little people. It aids in the exchange of information on medical treatment, employment, clothing, shoes, and education.

 National Information Center for Children and Youth with Disabilities
PO Box 1492
Washington, DC 22013
202-884-8200 (voice, TDD)
800-695-0285 (voice, TDD)
This center collects and shares information and ideas that are helpful to children and youth with disabilities and to people who care for and about them.

 National Association of the Physically Handicapped, Inc.
Bethesda Scarlet Oaks, No. GA4
440 Lafayette Avenue
Cincinnati, OH 45220-1000
513-961-8040
This association advances the social, economic, and physical welfare of persons who are physically handicapped in the U.S. and develops awareness of the needs of people who are physically disabled and supports legislation for their benefit.

❤ Administration on Developmental Disabilities
Office of Human Development Services
U.S. Department of Health and Human Services
200 Independence Avenue, SW
Washington, DC 20201
202-690-5504
202-245-2890
This office administers the Developmental Disabilities Assistance and
Bill of Rights Act, whose programs and services assist persons with
developmental disabilities to achieve independence, productivity, and
integration into the community.

❤ Paralyzed Veterans of America
801 18th Street NW
Washington, DC 20006
202-872-1300
This organization has excellent materials for persons who are wheelchair
users.

❤ Federation for Children with Special Needs
95 Berkeley Street, Suite 014
Boston, MA 02116
617-482-2915
413-562-5521
617-695-2939 fax
This is a coalition of eleven statewide parent organizations that act on
behalf of children and adults with a variety of special needs.

❤ National Alliance of Senior Citizens
1700 18th Street NW, Suite 401
Washington, DC 20009
202-986-0117
202-986-2974 fax
The Alliance advocates the advancement of senior Americans. It seeks
to inform the American public of the needs of senior citizens and of the
programs and policies being carried out by the government.

❤ National Association of Child Advocates
1625 K Street NW, Suite 510
Washington, DC 20006
202-828-6950
202-828-6956 fax
State organizations: 40. This association works for the safety, security,
health and education for all America's children by building and
supporting state and community-based independent child advocacy
organizations.

United Nations Children's Fund
3 United Nations Plz.
New York, NY 10017
1-800-FOR-KIDS
212-326-7000
UNICEF works for sustainable human development to ensure the survival, protection, and development of children around the world.

 National Easter Seal Society
230 West Monroe
Chicago, IL 60606
800-221-6827
312-726-1494 fax
This organization has excellent materials regarding architectural barriers and transportation of persons with disabilities and sponsors camps for family respite care.

## 8. Learning Differences

 Council for Learning Disabilities
PO Box 40303
Overland Park, KS 66204
913-492-8755
913-492-2546 fax
This council works with individuals who have learning disabilities and aids all LD educators in the exchange of information through publications and conferences.

 Learning Disabilities Association of America
4156 Library Road
Pittsburgh, PA 15234
412-341-1515
412-344-0224 fax
State chapters: 50. Local chapters: 750. This is a national information center and referral services with hundreds of affiliates. It offers a free information packet and publishes a newsletter and journal.

 National Center for Learning Disabilities
381 Park Avenue South, Suite 1420
New York, NY 10016
212-545-7510
This center provides financial support for research on learning disabilities.

# 9. Intellectual Differences

♦ National Association for Gifted Children
1707 L Street NW 550
Washington, DC 20036
202-785-4268
State Groups: 50. This association advances interest in programs for children who are gifted. It seeks to further educate those who are gifted and to enhance their potential creativity and Distributes information to teachers and parents on the development of the gifted child.

♦ American Association on Mental Retardation
444 North Capitol Street NW, Suite 846
Washington, DC 20001-1512
202-387-1968
800-424-3688
202-387-2193 fax
This is an interdisciplinary association of professionals and individuals concerned about the field of mental retardation. It promotes the well-being of individuals with mental retardation and supports those who work in the field.

♦ The Arc
http://TheArc.org
This Internet homepage provides a wealth of information on developmental delays and mental retardation, with numerous links to other areas of interest.

♦ American Mensa Limited
201 Main Street, Suite 1101
Ft. Worth, TX 76102
800-66MENSA
718-934-3700
This is a society for individuals who have established by score in a standard intelligence test that their intelligence is higher than that of 98% of the population.

♦ National Association for Creative Children and Adults
8080 Springvalley Drive
Cincinnati, OH 45236
513-631-1777
This association is a group of people that meet to share creative ideas and activities.

## 10. Health Diversity

 National Center for Health Education
72 Spring Street, Suite 208
New York, NY 10012-4019
212-334-9845 fax
This organization promotes health education in schools and manages a comprehensive school health education curriculum called "Growing Healthy."

 ODPHP National Health Information Center
PO Box 1133
Washington, DC 20013-1133
800-336-4797
301-565-4167
301-984-4256 fax
This center aids consumers in locating health information. The group is funded by the Office of Disease Prevention and Health Promotion, Public Health Service, Department of Health and Human Services.

 CDC National AIDS Clearinghouse
PO Box 6003
Rockville, MD 20849-6003
800-458-5231
Operated by the Center for Disease Control, this hotline provides current information about AIDS and HIV.

 National Organization for Rare Disorders
100 Rt. 37
PO Box 8923
New Fairfield, CT 06812
203-746-6518
203-746-6481 fax
203-746-6927 (TDD)
This is a clearinghouse for information on over 5,000 little-known disorders affecting some 20 million Americans. It is committed to the identification, treatment, and cure of rare disorders through programs of education, advocacy, research, and service.

 National Center for Chronic Disease Prevention and Health Promotion
http://www.social.com/health/nhic/data/hr000/hr0069.html
This Internet page provides information on prevention chronic diseases.

Association for the Care of Children's Health
7910 Woodmont Avenue, Suite 300
Bethesda, MD 20814
301-654-6549
301-986-4553 fax
This association advocates family-centered, psychosocially sound, and developmentally appropriate health care for children. It promotes meaningful collaboration among families and professionals across all disciplines to plan, coordinate, deliver, and evaluate children's health care systems.

 Epilepsy Foundation of America
4351 Garden City Drive
Landover, MD 20785
301-459-3700
800-332-1000 (information)
800-332-4050 (library)
301-577-2684 fax
This foundation is dedicated to the well-being of persons with epilepsy. It sponsors research and provides toll-free information to lay and professional inquirers. Local affiliates offer support groups, employment assistance, and other direct services.

 American Cancer Society
1599 Clifton Road NE
Atlanta, GA 30329
800-ACS-2345
404-320-3333
This is a nationwide voluntary health organization dedicated to eliminating cancer as a major health problem and preventing cancer, saving the lives of persons with cancer, and diminishing suffering through research, education, and service.

 Muscular Dystrophy Association
3300 East Sunrise Drive
Tucson, AZ 85718
520-529-2000
This association provides comprehensive patient care throughout its nationwide network of 230 MDA clinics. It also supports an international research program to find the causes and treatments for muscular dystrophy and related neuromuscular diseases.

American Lung Association
1740 Broadway
New York, NY 10019
212-315-8700
800-LUNG-USA
This association is dedicated to the conquest of lung disease and the promotion of lung health.

 Immune Deficiency Foundation
25 W. Chesapeake Avenue, Suite 206
Towson, MD 21204
410-321-6647
800-296-4499
410-321-9165 fax
This foundation supports research and education for the primary immune deficiency diseases and offers various publications on these diseases.

 Juvenile Diabetes Foundation International
120 Wall Street
New York, NY 10015-3904
212-889-7575
800-JDF-CURE
212-725-7259 fax
This is a voluntary health agency founded by parents of diabetic children who were convinced that, through research, diabetes could be cured.

 National Multiple Sclerosis Society
733 3rd Ave., Sixth Floor
New York, NY 10017
212-986-3240
212-986-7981 fax
This group funds research into causes and cures for MS, provides a variety of publications, and has local chapters throughout the country.


## 11. Communication Diversity

 Voice Foundation
1721 Pine Street
Philadelphia, PA 19103
215-735-7999
215-735-9293 fax
This foundation supports programs of professional education, scientific research, and public information essential to solving vocal problems.

♦ American Speech-Language-Hearing Association
10801 Rockville Pike
Rockville, MD 20852
800-638-8255
301-897-5700 (Voice or TDD)
This association provides information and referral on a broad range of
speech, language, and hearing disorders.

♦ National Center for Stuttering
200 East 33rd Street
New York, NY 10016
800-221-2483
212-532-1460
This center provides information to parents of children who stutter,
offers treatment for children and adults who stutter, and provides
training on the latest practices and theories for speech pathologists..

♦ Orton Dyslexia Society, Inc.
Chester Building, Suite 382
8600 LaSalle Road
Baltimore, MD 21286-2044
800-ABCD123
410-296-0232
410-321-5069 fax
This organization honors Samuel T. Orton, a physician who studied
children with language disorders. It combines the interests of both
medical and educational professionals interested in dyslexia and
language-learning disorders. It sponsors free referrals for diagnosis and
treatment. It also seeks to educate the public about dyslexia and
support efforts to enhance the self-worth of persons with dyslexia.

## 12. Behavior and Personality Diversity

♦ Autism Society of America
7910 Woodmont Avenue, Suite 650
Bethesda, MD 20814-3015
800-3-AUTISM
301-657-0881
301-657-0869 fax
Local chapters: 160. This is a national umbrella organization serving the
needs of autistic citizens of all ages. It provides information and
referrals to parents, professionals, and individuals.

Children and Adults with Attention Deficit Disorders
499 NW 70th Avenue, Suite 101
Plantation, FL 33317
305-587-3700
305-587-4599 fax
This is a national alliance of 625 parent organizations which provides information to parents of children with attention deficit disorders.

 Internet Psychology Resources
http://www.gasov.edu/psychweb/resource/bytopic.htm
This Internet homepage presents many topics on behavior, including autism, ADD, depression, and personality.


## 13. Sensory Diversity

 Alexander Graham Bell Association for the Deaf
3417 Volta Place NW
Washington, DC 20007
202-337-5220
This association of 17 state and 110 local groups encourages people with hearing impairments to communicate by developing maximal use of residual hearing, speech-writing, and speech and language skills.  It also promotes better public understanding of hearing loss in children and adults, and helps oral deaf adults and parents of hearing impaired children.

 National Association of the Deaf
814 Thayer Avenue
Silver Spring, MD 20910-4500
301-587-1788 (voice)
301-587-1789 (TDD)
This is the largest consumer organization of disabled persons in the United States, with more than 22,000 members and 51 affiliated state associations.  It serves as an advocate for the millions of deaf and hard-of-hearing people in America.

 American Council of the Blind
1155 15th Street NW, Suite 720
Washington, DC 20005
202-467-5081
The Council advocates legislation for persons who are blind.  Priority areas of advocacy include civil rights, social security and supplemental income, national health insurance, rehabilitation, eye research, and technology.

Association for the Education and Rehabilitation of the Blind and
Visually Impaired
206 N. Washington Street, Suite 320
Alexandria, VA 22314
703-548-1884
Regional Groups: 7. State Groups: 44. This is the only professional
membership organization dedicated to the advancement of education
and rehabilitation of children and adults who are blind and visually
impaired.

 Deaf-Blind Online
http://198.234.201.48/dbonline.html
This Internet homepage provides a list of pointers to informative
homepages dealing with visual and hearing impairments.


## 14. Family Perspectives

 Institute of Marriage and Family Relations
6116 Rolling Road, Suite 306
Springfield, VA 22152
703-569-2400
703-569-7248 fax
Offering professionally staffed diagnostic, treatment, counseling, and
education centers, this institute endeavors to assist individuals and
families in coping with and working through problems in family life and
relationships.

 Family Resource Coalition
200 South Michigan Avenue, Suite 1600
Chicago, IL 60604
312-341-0900
312-341-9361 fax
This is a national coalition of community-based family support
organizations concerned with parenting, family issues, child
development, education, and community life.

 American Federation of Teachers
555 New Jersey Avenue NW
Washington, DC 20001
800-238-1133
202-879-4400
202-879-4556 fax
Local Groups: 2,200. This federation assists teachers, educational
organizations, and community organizations to work effectively with
children.

National Council on Family Relations
3989 Central Avenue NE, Suite 550
Minneapolis, MN 55421
612-781-9331
612-781-9348 fax
Regional Groups: 3. State Groups: 41. This is a group of family life
professionals, including clergy, counselors, educators, home economists,
lawyers, nurses, librarians, physicians, psychologists, social workers,
sociologists, and researchers. It seeks to advance marriage and family
life through consultation, conferences, and the dissemination of
information and research. The group specializes in family health issues,
ethnic minorities, and religion and family life.

 National Education Association
1201 16th Street NW
Washington, DC 20036
202-833-4000
202-822-7621 fax
State Groups: 53. Local Groups: 12,000. This is a professional
organization and union of elementary, secondary, college and university
teachers, as well as administrators, principals, counselors, and others
concerned with education. Special committees address civil rights,
minority affairs, international relations, and women's concerns.